PROFILES IN SOCIAL WORK

SOCIAL WORK SERIES

The Practice of Clinical Casework
  G. Sackheim, M.S.

Social Work Research in Human Services
  H. Wechsler, Ph.D., H. Z. Reinherz, S.M., M.S. Hyg., Sc.D.,
  and D. D. Dobin, M.S.W.

Profiles in Social Work
  M. Gottesfeld, M.S.S. and M. Pharis, M.S.W.

Foster Home Care
  A. R. Gruber, D.S.W.

Social Work Ethics
  C. Levy, D.S.W.

Social Work with Children
  F. Lieberman, D.S.W.

PROFILES IN SOCIAL WORK

WITHDRAWN

Mary L. Gottesfeld
and Mary E. Pharis

HUMAN SCIENCES PRESS
Formerly *BEHAVIORAL PUBLICATIONS INC.*
72 FIFTH AVENUE, NEW YORK, N.Y. 10011

Library of Congress Catalog Number 76-20697

ISBN: 0-87705-296-4

Copyright © 1977 by Human Sciences Press
72 Fifth Avenue, New York, New York 10011

Printed in the United States of America
6789   987654321
Library of Congress Cataloging in Publication Data

Library of Congress Cataloging in Publication Data
Main entry under title:
    Profiles in social work.
    Consists mainly of transcripts of interviews.
    Bibliography: p.
    1. Social workers—United States—Interviews.
2. Social service—United States. I. Gottesfeld,
Mary. II. Pharis, Mary E.
HV91.P76 361'.973 76-20697

CONTENTS

PREFACE

This is a book about social work leaders. Social work exploits its best people. In addition to their demanding, full-time positions as teachers, writers, and practitioners, throughout their careers the leaders interviewed for this book have been invited to give countless summer institutes, lectures, and seminars and to chair symposia. Their books and articles are read, their views solicited, their energies drained by a profession hungry for their insights.

Unless we wish to view social work's heavy demand on their time and intellect as a distorted form of esteem, we must conclude that the profession does little to honor its finest sons and daughters and still less to know them as people. This book is intended, first and foremost, to honor eight of social work's outstanding leaders and, in addition, to offer the contemporary social worker a glimpse of them as human beings. They are remarkable human beings indeed.

We do not in any way view these eight individuals as forming an inclusive group of social work leaders. We selected them by the unsystematic but thoroughly pleasant method of requesting interviews with those who were best known to us by reputation and with whom we were able to arrange time for interviews during 1974 and 1975. Although we hope to interview other social workers, known and unknown, in the future, for the moment we honor these eight.

With the obvious exception of Jane Addams, whose "comments" are derived largely from her own books and articles, each man and woman spoke with us for a minimum of two hours, and the interviews were fully taped and transcribed. Every effort has been made to edit the conversations as little as possible so that the individual's personal, informal style of speaking would be retained. Thus, on occasion, syntax has been sacrificed on behalf of essential meaning. Our hope is that each individual's personality as well as viewpoint would emerge more fully in colloquial exchange. In other words, honoring and learning to know our leaders were the primary objectives of this book. But as we talked with these men and women and as we read and reread their transcripts, it became more and more clear to us that through them, we might also be able to help the profession understand *itself* better.

Why did social work come to admire these particular men and women? Surely when an individual rises to a position of leadership within any profession, that fact alone indicates that he has exceptional abilities, qualities that are highly valued by his professional peers. Conversely, it indicates something about the profession: its leaders themselves *reflect* those values that the profession holds dear at any given moment. In this sense, it can be said that, to some degree, the selection of leadership within any profession is a kind of transference phenomenon. Insofar as this is so, then these leaders tell us something about our profession, just as they tell us something about their own lives. Understanding these interviews in that light may be as important as honoring and coming to know the men and women who granted them.

Chapter 1

SOCIAL WORK: A PSYCHOSOCIAL HISTORY

What do the eight men and women who were interviewed for this book tell us about ourselves and our history? For one thing, they tell us something about social work's growth and scope. When Jane Addams was born—during the first year of the Civil War—the profession of social work did not exist. There were no schools of social work, no organizations of people who functioned as social workers. America was an agrarian nation of 31 million people; the average lifespan was approximately 43 years.

When Jane Addams confounded the statistics on life expectancy by dying a full 74 years later in 1935, social work was a well-established, growing, exciting young profession. There were now 127 million Americans who could expect to live an average of 60 years. That same year, Fritz Redl received an invitation from the Rockefeller Foundation which would bring him to the United States and mark the beginning of his long association with social work. Florence Hollis had received her MSS at Smith four years before; Helen Perlman had just earned her certificate as a Commonwealth Fellow at the New York School of Social Work and was about to marry. Yonata Feldman, who had known Jane Addams, was already established in her own career by 1935 and was teaching and training social workers in New York at the Jewish Board of Guardians; young James Dumpson was teaching in the Pennsylvania public school system while considering whether he should enter graduate school in social work. Selma Fraiberg was about to enroll at Wayne State University as a freshman, and Virginia Satir was 18 years old and only a year away from college graduation.

So we see that social work's heritage is far from a lengthy one, however varied and rich it may seem to us. When the eight leaders were studying, teaching, and rising to prominence, the *professional* core of social work was still remarkably small. In the year Jane Addams died—which was also the year this nation's first Social Security Act became law—there were only 31 graduate schools of social work, producing perhaps 950 MSWs a year, and this in a nation of 127 million with over 10 million unemployed. (Forty years after Miss Addam's death, almost three times as many graduate schools are producing six times as many MSWs annually.)

It becomes evident that in choosing social work, these men and women were hardly seeking job or career security. They wanted to work with people who were hurting; in most cases it was as simple and amorphous as that. They were affiliating themselves, not so much with an established, structured, socially visible profession, as with a system of activities that was united by an interest in helping people.

In Jane Addams's Hull House days, there was no theory of helping. To be sure, there was commitment, and often it was cast in a religious mold. But the emerging social problems of the late 1800s and early 1900s, spawned by increasing industrialization and urbanization and seasoned by massive immigration, were new problems, not only to America, but to the world. Early social workers—those bold or foolish men and women who chose to wrestle with these problems—had no convenient theories to help them plan their activities. Nowhere in the world were there tried-and-true programs of social support or legislated provisions for the general welfare. Although Bismarck had experimented in Germany with social programming and the Fabian Society of the Webbs, and George Bernard Shaw in England was arguing with wit and precision against the groundswell of social Darwinism that sought to justify blatant injustice, Americans who would help their fellow man had no legislation and little helping theory to rely on (aside from religious injunction, much of which was contradictory). The settlement houses and the Charity Organization Societies and their early efforts at in-service training, which in fact constituted the first social work education, were rooted in doing, as best they could, whatever work was most forcefully thrust upon them.

So we find that the infant profession which turned to these eight leaders for direction was, in its early days, young, unstructured, broad in scope, vague in delimitation, starved for useful theory, and lacked conventional status or sanction. These leaders chose a career affiliation with social work, perhaps not so much in spite of these limitations as because of them. For, as we believe the interviews themselves suggest, these people are comfortable with, even excited by unusually loose confines of self-identification. As the social work profession labored steadily to clarify its professional image through professional organization, development of curriculum and degree sequences, endorsement of ethical codes, and the like, these leaders consistently declined to be hemmed in by whatever definitional limits emerged.

Satir says "Don't box me in," and Redl tells us he hates labels and refuses to label himself. Fraiberg is a researcher, educator, psychoanalyst, *and* a social worker. Feldman, Satir, and Dumpson taught children before they taught social workers, and all three have carried educational and administrative as well as direct service responsibility. Hollis and Perlman are writers and teachers as much as they are social workers (indeed, the Bureau of Labor Statistics does *not* categorize professors of social work as social workers). These people are social workers, and they are much more than social workers.

Herein lies a paradox for the profession. Social work has chosen, and held up to its members for inspiration and emulation, many leaders and models who cannot and will not be conveniently boxed into the limits of the field as it is conventionally defined, no matter how vague the definition. In part this phenomenon is explained by the fact that all our subjects have been practitioners or, to use a more generic term, psychotherapists. To be a good psychotherapist—or caseworker or group therapist—one must partake of many disciplines. A good psychotherapist should have a broad education in the humanities as well as in social work, psychology, biology, sociology, and the like. You will observe this when you read about the literary familiarity of Perlman and Fraiberg, Feldman's early training in philology, the knowledge of history and the ability to integrate it shown by Satir, Redl, Hollis, and Dumpson. Their interests range widely through the many educational facets that contribute to the making of a good therapist and also defy a more narrow educational mold.

In addition to their broad and flexible self-identifications, these uncommon people have other characteristics in common. Well-traveled and sophisticated men and women of the world though they are, each retains and even cultivates within himself or herself an element of ethnicity, or provinciality, or perhaps a sense of difference or distinctness within our broader culture. Two were immigrants. Four are Jews. One is black and a Catholic. Satir recalls the impact of her remote and rural Wisconsin upbringing. Perlman tells of being advised that as a Jew and a woman she could have no career in academia. Feldman recounts her struggle against the multiple barriers of being an intelligent female and a Jew striving for education in repressive Imperial Russia. Each has integrated the sense of difference as a valuable part of the past. No doubt this characteristic is closely related to the ease with which each eschews a precise professional identification in the present. Just as these leaders are at ease being many things at once in the present, so did they learn to be comfortable with their own ethnic, social, racial, or foreign wellsprings in the past.

Interestingly, each one is specific, generous, and genuine in acknowledging teachers and mentors in social work. How many graduate social work students today will acknowledge, 20 or 30 years from now, any specific social work teacher with the feeling and enthusiasm that these people do? Social work training in the twenties, thirties, and forties was still *field* training primarily: an intimate, personal, individual experience. We can see the tremendous impact of the teaching-learning relationships in the recollections of these leaders and in their expressions of affection and collegial gratitude. Even today, there is universal recognition among social work students and many of their teachers that the field work experience and the supervision of that experience is the cornerstone of a genuine grasp of social work theory and practice, the single most essential experience in education for social work.

But the great social work educator Charlotte Towle might grieve to see what has happened to the student of this profession today. In the push for academic legitmacy and in the face of student uneasiness in the tutorial structure of the experience, social work has diluted and restructured its fieldwork programs. Few academic settings today *require* a student to engage over a two-year period in a consistent, intensive, case-by-case and interview-by-interview, individually supervised fieldwork experience. Furthermore, fewer students entering the field are interested in such intimate and effective learning.

The leaders we interviewed acknowledge their debt to significant teachers as well as others who influenced them because they were individually *touched* by their learning experiences. They were trained in small classes by teachers who actually practiced, felt less pressed to obtain tenure, and felt more pressed to advance understanding of how to help. That meant understanding people. It may be that the growth in the profession's size has made it impossible to recapture the experience of the more intimate and personal apprenticeship quality of early social work education. Unquestionably, expansion has occurred at the cost of diminishing the fieldwork experience. Hollis cogently delineates this part of our history. Thus we must ask ourselves whether we have deprived ourselves of the fertile soil that gave us the kind of individuals we interviewed for this book.

All the contemporary leaders we have interviewed to date seem to have been profoundly affected in their social work beginnings by the era of "psychiatric deluge." Although argument has developed with regard to when, precisely, the influence of psychoanalytic theory so firmly seized the profession, there is little argument that it did so. Indeed, with the possible exception of literary artists, in the thirties, forties, and fifties social workers proved to be the single most receptive audience for psychoanalytic theory. Sigmund Freud was born four years before Jane Addams was and died four years after she did; they were contemporaries. When Freud gave his American lectures on psychoanalysis at Clark University in 1910, Jane Addams had already begun her second 20 years at Hull House. No doubt she and her remarkable colleagues had discovered limitations in their approach. Although they had had impressive successes with the poor and immigrant ghetto families they lived among, they had failures too—often puzzling, unexpected, and frustrating failures.

So, leaving the individual casework effort to the corps of younger workers they had trained, the leaders of Hull House focused their energies increasingly on issues of national and organizational scope: legislation for child and maternal health, protective regulations for the laboring man, the peace movement, and the like. Thus it was among the ranks of those who still dealt with cases on a one-to-one or familial basis, not those who turned to legislative and organizational efforts, that psychoanalytic theory took hold.

The phenomenon demands explanation. Although the psychiatric era in social work may seem quaint and foolish to many present-day social workers, and others view this singularly prominent feature in our professional history with hostility and disgust, the fact is that for perhaps half of its life-span as a profession, social work drew continually and almost exclusively from one increasingly elaborate theoretical resource. It is of great importance to know why.

In large part, social work embraced analytic theory because certain practical limits had been attained for the moment in other social work endeavors. By the early years of the twentieth century, many social workers had already become skilled and imaginative manipulators of environmental variables. Life was less complex, and the sphere in which things could be done on behalf of any individual or family was certainly smaller. The resources of relatives and the neighborhood could be mobilized, the few available (private) charity and educational resources tapped, and appropriate moral or technical instruction offered. To supplement these skills, social work had quite appropriately turned to lobbying for more protective and supportive legislation on behalf of individuals and families. But following the era of reform at the turn of the century and Teddy

Roosevelt's genuine efforts to ease the abuses wrought by industrialization, the nation devoted itself first to avoiding and then to immersing itself in World War I while social action on behalf of the needy of our society waited. The wait lengthened as America enjoyed the heady and narcissistic twenties, and social workers continued to manipulate environments, hope and work for social change, and puzzle over those who seemed unreached by these approaches.

Thwarted as they were for almost 30 years by their inability to achieve pervasive social reform, it is little wonder that practitioners grew discouraged in their efforts to modify from the one end of the continuum, through change in external social modifications. Many began to develop their abilities and skills to modify the other end, individual behavior. Frustrated in the effort to change their clients' external circumstances, caseworkers sought to increase their options to change clients' internal situation *beyond* those personal changes that seemed to occur through direct injunctive education and environmental manipulation. The field needed tools to be better able to help; if the tools were not readily found in changing the society, many in the field concluded that psychoanalytic theory offered the best promise for providing them. If one could understand human behavior better, one could help better. Feldman describes this phenomenon quite graphically.

It seems important to note that the contemporary leaders we interviewed are not *products* of the psychoanalytic era; they are far from passive, uncritical consumers of psychoanalytic theory. Nor was the theory, we should recall, a neat, coherent, elaborated monolith. Rather, these men and women, free as they were to test out and try on new and amorphous ideas, just as they had tested and tried on a new and amorphous profession, *utilized* the theory's offerings. Without exception, our leaders demonstrate originality and a creative ability to integrate and apply ideas, new and old. Redl's great contribution has been his clinical understanding of group psychology and his use of it in work with disturbed children; Feldman displays a knowledge of Freud and also of Rank, Federn, and great modern theorists such as Spotnitz; Hollis and Perlman are jointly famous for their seminal contributions to casework theory; Dumpson's work in the development of a landmark treatment approach to delinquent children preceded his complex administrative positions; Fraiberg's classic work in child development has evolved into a special interest in the development of blind infants and children; Satir is both a trail blazer and an innovator in the area of family therapy.

Again and again, these people prove their bold iconoclasm. They were not and are not blind, puristic "true believers." Administrator Dumpson calls for welfare workers who really understand human relationships, just as therapist Fraiberg calls for child welfare legislation! They can unify polar extremes. If they are united by any one characteristic, it is their distaste for orthodoxy—of any sort. Their horizons have remained open.

In contrast, social work as a whole has always tended somewhat to foreclose its options and views prematurely. Rather than let time and the natural dialectic work to refine ideas and techniques continuously, the main body of the profession has been perhaps too eager to solidify, and stultify, social work skill and knowledge. As a result, we have witnessed the astoundingly fevered and foolish functional-diagnostic controversy, fought as though only one view could prevail as "truth." We have seen the equally ridiculous dichotomization of practice techniques into environmental manipulation *or* psychodynamic intervention, as though they were discrete and unrelated entities. The profession as a whole, far less able to integrate polar extremes than are these leaders, continues even today to clump itself into camps: community organizer versus direct service personnel, activist versus clinician, MSW versus BA worker, black versus white. Each group behaves as though it alone has access to some final professional truth.

Why did the psychiatric era come upon such hard times in the profession? There are many reasons. Perhaps today's razzle-dazzle culture demands more mechanistic and supposedly rapid techniques and a technocracy to sustain the illusion of a more effective attack on today's problems of more massive scale. For years, the direct-service practitioner had no place to go in the profession if he wished to work with people. Because there was no private practice of social work, assertive and talented people within the profession were forced to move up and out of the sphere in which analytic theory was most obviously relevant: direct practice. Then too, as Hollis suggests, many caseworkers who *did* fully invest themselves in the psychoanalytic movement within social work were often content with their interesting work; they refused deanships and administrative roles and thus permitted others to come to the professional fore.

Whatever the explanations, the field is certainly changing. As social work seems to turn to a new set of "truths" and to new orthodoxies of community action and social advocacy, who are its leaders and what precisely are its tools? The profession seems as unsure of itself in the 1970s as to what, exactly, employing the tools of activism means as it must have been in the 1930s when it pondered what employing the tools of psychodynamic treatment meant.

The men and women in this book, unorthodox and inconoclastic to the last, do not seem to share the discomfort caused by this confusion. They know what they are up to; they have paid their money and taken their chances and seem rather satisfied with where they have been and where they are going. After interviewing them, we came away with an impression of their excellence and their tremendous energy and enthusiasm for their own spheres of interest. They value social work and what it has given them, and they wish it well. But if it heads in directions that seem irrelevant to them, they do not feel compelled to follow. They reflect very nearly the full span of the profession's existence, and they have taught us much. It would be a shame to part company with any of them.

One thing our leaders clearly seem to lack is that pervasive sense of inferiority so often attached to the label "social worker." Satir makes a direct reference to this point while blithely ignoring professional boundaries when she observes that all mental health practitioners need "to know the same things." How is it that these people seem to accept so easily that "social work is beautiful" while so many of the rank and file seek to deny their origins, often by taking other titles (e.g., administrator, psychoanalyst, social psychotherapist)? It seems clear that we are not an honored profession in this society because, in the minds of many, we are identified with our clients. We are willing to work with the underprivileged and the unfortunate, who are always suspect in a society that fundamentally believes that almost everyone on the welfare rolls could take themselves off if they had more appreciation of the "work ethic." Furthermore, to be altruistic is to be effete and unaggressive, presumed characteristics that are neither admired nor financially rewarded. In short, American society is ambivalent about professional social work. Philanthropy is good but "bleeding hearts" are bad. This ambivalence, we believe, is at the root of public attitudes toward social work.

At the end of his interview, Fritz Redl says: "In social work we had a beautiful concept of the 'professional self,' remember that?" In reading about these leaders it is clear that they have never forgotten this concept. To emulate them would be—first and foremost—to be a dedicated professional. Because they are our leaders, their work represents our profession to the public, and this is why we should achieve more professionalization in social work, not less. Our clients deserve more, not less, and only by being completely professional, not by deprofessionalizing, can we produce new generations of men and women such as these. In this way, we are not merely elevating our profession; we can also speak credibly and forcefully on social issues, as we are qualified to do, and can insure that those who are designated as social workers are competent.

If there emerge genuine psychodynamic themes, then, in social work's selection of its leaders—themes that may show us what we have valued—perhaps they are the following:

- We have sought leaders who showed us they are free, free in the sense of being unconfined by conventional limits or theoretical orthodoxy. These leaders hold their beliefs, but are not "believers." They have changed and grown. They will not be labeled.

- We have admired men and women who treasure their own ethnicity, their own sense of being different from all others. We want to learn, as they have, to integrate our identities as both separate and together with others. Erikson would say these individuals teach us that one must identify with both "my kind" and "mankind."

- We have learned from our leaders that we must not choose to polarize: we need to know both the internal needs and dynamics of people and the external demands of the world. They are integral: there can be no profit in taking sides. The best social workers are able to grasp the whole man in his world.

- We have discovered again from these men and women that learning can never be solely academic or cerebral. These are "feelingful" people who learned within relationships of remarkable depth. They remind us that learning is visceral and emotional as well as intellectual, an intimate and total endeavor.

We see that social work has wanted leaders, and its own common man, to be able to bridge gaps: gaps in communication, gaps in culture and class, gaps in theory and values. To do this, the leader, or any social worker, must really know interior man; human interactive behavior; the realities of social, economic and political life; *and* himself. He must know them all at one and the same time, and he must know them well. We believe the interviews in this book reflect that the profession esteems such ideals and the individuals who have consistently strived to attain them.

Excellence is by definition a rare thing. But what if all social workers reached for such values with the success that these few leaders have? A profession whose main body had achieved them would, we must assume, be genuinely effective in dealing with human needs on an individual, group, and community basis. It would be a profession tolerant of differences within itself and of colleagues with divergent interests and beliefs. We leave it to you to decide whether contemporary social work is reaching for the levels of professional maturity it so admires in its individual leaders.

JANE ADDAMS (1860–1935) was the founder of Hull House in Chicago and in 1931 was awarded the Nobel Peace Prize.

Chapter 2

JANE ADDAMS

In the 40 years since your death, you have become more of a symbol to Americans, and especially to American social workers, than any other woman in the social services, past or present. For most of us now, you are more legendary than real.

Perhaps they no longer read the books and articles that I wrote; I think I come through as real enough in them, though I grant that writing styles have changed.

Would you tell us a bit about your background? You say your-self that "one's bent may be tracked back to the 'No-Man's Land' where character is formless" in childhood (1910, p. 1). What was your childhood like?

Objectively speaking, I had an exceedingly comfortable childhood. My father was a remarkable man, a Quaker, a man of tremendously sensitive and humanistic orientation but exceedingly practical as well. He was an early settler and businessman, a miller and a banker in Illinois, and by the time I was born in 1860, he was the leading citizen of Cedarville. Basically, he was a somber, philosophic man, psychologically kin to Lincoln, who was his friend and with whom he corresponded. But he had great worldly success as well: he was for 16 years an Illinois state senator, and on one occasion he turned down the nomination and what would have been the certain election to the governorship of Illinois. By the time he died, when I was 21, he was a leading citizen in the state.

I had been his eighth child, but only four of us grew to maturity. My mother died before I have memory of her, when I was two and a half. My father remarried, but not until I was eight, so for the fullest part of my childhood I was his youngest child and the recipient of his tenderest affections. I was fully devoted to him, in awe of him, in love with him, and in constant fear that I might fail to live up to his exceptional standards, which were early transmitted to me as principle, whether I could uphold them or not.

Christopher Lasch (1965, pp. 17–18) *suggests you were committed to your father's "unyielding masculine example."*

The comment has some merit. But then, given the fact that at a most crucial time of my development, I had no other example, no mother or feminine model, save for the ladies of Cedarville, perhaps it is not necessary to emphasize the masculine aspect. It is true that evermore I retained my father's commitment to principle, his assertiveness, and I hope also his practicality.

In Twenty Years At Hull House (1910, pp. 11 and 52), *you mention two tragic events, the deaths of your mother and your father, each in only a single sentence.*

Yes. One does not write elaborately on the deepest of wounds. You see, objectively as a child I was secure, as I have said, but subjectively I was not. I was a shy child who felt entirely unworthy of my exceptional father. In that same book, I called myself an Ugly Duckling, and I felt I was. I long wrestled with a conscience that indicted me for each small, childhood lie, and I was subject, too, to fearful dreams. In one, I dreamed night after night that everyone in the world was dead excepting myself and that upon me rested the responsibility of making a wagon wheel. I did not know how to begin, although I fully realized that the affairs of the world could not be resumed until at least one wheel should be made and something started (1910, p. 5).

How did you find your way out of such tense and somber thoughts and feelings?

I did not, for a very long time. Oh, when my father remarried, (then I was eight), the widow, Mrs. George Haldeman, brought her two sons. And my stepbrother George, who was only six months younger than I, was to be a great boon to me. We became devoted to one another; he cultivated my interest in science, and until I went away to Rockford College and he to Beloit, we were inseparable. He was, unknowingly, a great balm to my seriousness, and he provided a needed alternative to the intimacy in which I had been cloistered with my father. Then, too, my childhood insecurities were eased by my college experiences.

You had wanted to go east to Smith College, hadn't you?

Yes. But my father preferred that I attend Rockford, where my older three sisters had matriculated. He felt that an education at a respectable midwestern institution, rounded out by a year in Europe upon graduation, as had been the pattern for my three sisters, would provide equal or greater advantage to the usual fine education at an eastern school. No doubt he was right; I never regretted it much. Rockford was good for me. I was given a very sound classical education; became acquainted with the most excellent young ladies, such as Ellen Gates Starr; began to develop some skills in debate (did you know I once debated William Jennings Bryan in a general contest in which we both lost!) and in writing, as the editor of the *Rockford Seminary Magazine.* I was active and respected, and I did well; it was much help to my sense of self-esteem and confidence.

In 1881 you graduated as valedictorian from Rockford.

It was to be the highlight of my young life to that time and was to remain so for years. Only weeks after that salubrious event, my father died quite suddenly. Whereupon began the worst period of my life. I was greatly depressed and grew more so with the passing days. Though I did begin at the Woman's Medical College in Philadelphia that fall and was doing well academically, my spirits failed, and my physical condition as well, within a year. I had a flare-up of a spinal condition and had sucessful surgery in 1882 but did not fully recover for years. I felt almost as though I could not be well—as though I had to do penance for my improved self-confidence and the development of my ambitions which had occurred while I was at Rockford, almost as though my father's death had been punishment for my hubris.

Is it true that you learned at the time of that surgery in 1882 that you could never have children?

Yes, that is what my stepbrother, Dr. Harry Haldeman, who performed the surgery, told me. I know it exacerbated my depression, with which I had struggled since my father's death. I sank into a state of dejection and self-loathing which stretched into eight years and echoed in my life even beyond that.

Not even the conventional prescription of the day for malaise, the European tour, could ease my spiritual discomfort and my sense of futility, even after my physical condition was once again satisfactory. Actually, the richness of the European adventure, against the richness of my background and education, grew more and more stultifying; the contrast of that richness against my uselessness and indecision at that time only deepended my lassitude. I later wrote of this: "You do not know what life means when all the difficulties are removed! I am simply smothered and sickened with advantages" (1910, p. 73).

The advantages of your excellent family heritage and education?

And too, the comfortable estate my father left. I shared in $350,000, which in 1881 was indeed an exceptional economic base. Without that, I could not have started Hull House, which was to be my salvation from the nervous exhaustion in which I languished for those eight dreadful years.

What, then, did bring you, a woman of moderate wealth in those times—well-educated, cultured, and sophisticated—to the momentous decision to found a settlement in a slum? It cannot really have been the famous bullfight episode alone, can it?

Why not? By that April of 1888, I had tried the elegant life in Baltimore society at my stepmother's suggestion. I had refused her other behest that I marry her son, my dear stepbrother and childhood companion, George. I had tried European tours and Christian baptism. I was filled with shame that in my 28 years I had not yet contributed one whit to the betterment of the world or of my fellow man.

Is that what you meant when you wrote: "I have seen young girls suffer and grow sensibly lowered in vitality in the first years after they leave school. In our attempt then to give a girl pleasure and freedom from care we succeed, for the most part, in making her pitifully miserable"? (1910, p. 118).

Yes, of course. I meant myself as much as any of my contemporaries. And in my continuing depression, I had begun the second round of curative tours. That Spring in Madrid, I sat transfixed for hours watching the methodical, ceremonial slaughter of five bulls and many more horses without feeling. As though in a dream, that evening it came to me that I *must* begin to act, or I should be forever lost, as I had been lost those prior eight years. I had long had a secret Hull House daydream; the bullfight awakened me to action.

Were you, in that one moment, so clearly found? Or is your recollection of this event supercharged in some way?

What you nowadays call a screen memory? Hm. It *was* on an Easter Sunday, the day of the Resurrection, mine as well as Christ's. It may be. All I know is that after years of inaction and moral stagnation, I began to move and to act once again. Within the 18 months, Hull House was founded: on the 18th of September 1889, my former Rockford classmate, Ellen Gates Starr, and I moved into the old Hull mansion on Halsted Street in Chicago. It was a great day for me: the end of my period of taking sustenance from society and the beginning of my time of giving back.

I don't want to take time from our interview for the specific history of Hull House itself. But would it be fair to say that the House was the device through which you found yourself and prepared yourself to move on to even greater social commitments?

I think so. Over the many years, the House did immeasurable service and is still doing a remarkable job in a variety of facilities in Chicago, although, of course, the Hull mansion itself is inactive now and affiliated with the school of social work at the University of Illinois.

Yes, the Jane Addams School of Social Work. And the House was saved from destruction largely through the efforts of social workers who demanded it as a memorial to you.

But the service it gave the folk of our neighborhood in my day was no greater than the service its founding did for me, I think.

You see, it was an era of great cultural crisis, as one author has called it (Lasch, 1965, p. 36), just as yours is also an era of cultural crisis in which the youth, like the children of the immigrants in my day, turn away from the values and patterns of their parents. Why? Because they are convinced they must find new ways to survive in a world vastly different from the parents' old world. It will happen with each new generation now, you know. Technology makes a new world in less than a generation now, duplicating for every child the necessity of denial of a parent's life-style. In my own cultural crisis, my turning from the comfort and ease of my existence and from my depression, Hull House was the method by which I discovered myself. As all good social work clinicians know, depression responds to real work in the world.

Let me ask you about social work. Did you think of yourself as a social worker?

Of course! I always spoke and wrote of myself as a social worker. I had the honor of being the first woman president of the National Conference of Social Work in 1909. I served on the board of the National Federation of Settlements until I died. Does anyone doubt that I was a social worker?

I only asked because a feeling of allegiance to the social work profession, as such, was rare around the turn of the century. After all, the first professional school of social work only opened its doors in 1904.

In my day, our professors were the poor themselves.

Would you, if you were training for the profession today, select a particular method?

It would be a difficult choice. All my work, even the legislative work and the work in support of the trade union movement, was grounded in what I observed happening to people—real people, one by one. We did casework at Hull House: delivered babies, counseled prostitutes, encouraged frightened but determined union organizers, worked with delinquents, even wrapped the dead for burial. I did all those things myself in my day. We made home visits but did not call them that. I never wrote an article or gave a speech that did not call upon my acquaintance with real people.

But many of Hull House's activities were developed and carried out in a group-work context, as was the case for all settlements. Our day nursery (it was our first community service) and our art and music and theater groups, our reading and sewing gatherings, our clubs for children in the afternoons and language classes for the immigrants in the evenings, our college courses (we were an extension of the University of Chicago), these were all clearly more kin to group work. I always liked work with groups.

As a leader?

Not only that. I liked to be in the group as well. I could follow. Often others took the lead in a number of the group efforts in which I was involved. The establishment of the Cook County Juvenile Court, for example—the first juvenile court in the world—was an effort in which my colleague Mrs. Bowen was clearly the leader.

Wasn't the founding of the Juvenile Court a community organization effort?

Yes. So Perhaps if I were in training today, I would be as drawn to the community organization method as the other two. It is still in its infancy as an official social work method, but much of my success at Hull House and with later organizations hinged on community organization principles and interests. Money—you had to get money for your cause and attract the influential people. And since we made it a policy to refuse money with questionable connections, or where there seemed to be unfortunate strings attached, the task became all the more difficult. And the community organization responsibility in terms of educating the communities! I spent enormous amounts of time and energy touring and lecturing, once I had gained some understanding of various cultures, generations, and district issues as well as the political mechanisms and money flow of the urban area. Informing the city and the nation became a major task.

I was, you see, all three: caseworker, group worker, community organizer. Can any social worker really serve only *one* role? I find it hard to believe. I suppose if I were in training now, I should be forced by my catholicity of interest to take one of those generic sequences and hope for the best.

Oh my! And we had hoped you'd endorse clinical work.

I do endorse it! But I don't think my own greatest skill lay in the clinicial area. We did not have your theory base, you know; and please don't ever forget how important a theory base is, even one that has failings. A base in theory is like strength of character: it must be there underpinning all the social worker's efforts, whether the worker is conscious of them or no, else the work comes to little. What good I was able to do on a casework basis came from my character, I suppose, for I often failed to understand individual behavior. With all the others of my social work generation, I thought that careful moral instruction might go far in alleviating the grief of many of my neighborhood's residents. Often it did, too. But not often did I understand why.

I want to ask if you feel that your program—the range of social services offered by the Hull House of your day—would be as relevant today. You wrote of the classes in Dante and Browning and mathematics, a Plato club, a series of lectures by John Dewey, a Shakespeare seminar, the Hull House Theatre, and many others. These programs might be successful in many a suburban community center, but would they sell in a contemporary urban ghetto?

We operated on entirely different assumptions and with an entirely different population, but even then we held our educational efforts to be totally subordinate to the *social* services of the House. Do you not think that any urban ghetto of today would welcome a free child care center? A low-cost group residence? We fed the hungry of our district and sold democracy 75 years ago; your Black Panthers at their most successful fed black children as a social service together with an indoctrination to their pinciples. Imaginative social workers can still adapt the settlement ideal when individualizing programs for your poor ghetto millions. The problem is not the adaptability of the programs! Indeed, the current avant-garde thinking about social services within the government itself now turns to the concept of community service centers to which citizens in *any* need may turn to find appropriate services.

The problem, it seems to me, lies in a lack of interest in getting in and doing it. You still have millions of people below the poverty level: actually, over 25 million. But it seems almost as if it is now thought that a governmental program alone, dollars alone, will solve that persistent social problem. Like your other recent remote-control wars, your War on Poverty has been managed at a distance. No, it is not failure of program that needs remedy in today's social services, it is failure of attitude and intent. Your ghettos could be reached if you wanted badly enough to reach them.

You sound as though you might favor the efforts of our young radical social workers.

Well, I never thought much of Marxism (though I was several times under severe censure and even, at one time, blacklisted by a Senate committee for my efforts to protect the civil rights of so-called subversives). But I do think that young people who call for getting in and knowing the poor are on the right track. As I once said: "A young person possessed with a fine enthusiasm for a new social program may work along side with the most careful social workers. . . . But he must do it all with his feet on the ground. He must not do it from an *a priori* conception of what society might and ought to be. He must know his congested neighborhood and give reasons for the faith which is in him. He need not mount a box on the street corner and preach a new social order, but he must be able to say to the people about him, in regard to the street which needs to be cleaned, that he knows the best method of procedure in order to bring about these reforms. And with that backing of careful neighborhood understanding and with definite relations to the city or state or federal government he may be as radical as he likes on the economic side [Johnson, 1960, p. 88]."

You mention Marxism, which brings to mind your trip to Russia, your visit with Tolstoy, and also your work for international peace.

Along with Hull House, my most important work was for the Woman's International League for Peace and Freedom.

I know you won the Nobel Peace Prize in 1931, even while you were being reviled in America as a traitor for your work on behalf of conscientious objectors in World War I and against that war as a whole. What can you say about the prospects for peace in the world now?

They appear to be not much better than in my time, which certainly isn't good. And, of course, peace is now more imperative than in my day. I am again deeply disappointed with America, much as I was regarding her failure to participate in the League of Nations, for which many of us worked so hard. If I had been alive at the time, I think Vietnam would have been the death of me!

Ms. Addams. . . .

I should be glad to have you call me Miss Addams or Jane. I am content to have known what the world already knows in any case: that I died a spinster at 74. If Ms. is designed to ease feelings of discomfort over that state, it is not necessary—unless it is you who may be uneasy about it. I am not.

But you were the single most outstanding spokeswoman for what was called, even in 1900, the Women's Movement, an outstanding feminist. Wouldn't you be active in the women's movement of today?

Indeed I would! It is merely that the form of address is to me of no significance. I was always less concerned with symbols than with realistic programs and accomplishments. It seems to me that the protests and social movements of your era are considerably more enamored of symbols, clever ploys, and catchy public relations in general than with substantial achievement on practical and political levels. But no matter. Yes, I am most excited by your current Women's Liberation Movement. I have the advantage of being able to recall what it was like to be without the vote. Women, and their civilizing influence on their families and on society in general, may be one of the greatest hopes for the future. I am entirely in favor of the National Organization for Women and would be a member if I were alive.

You know, most of the women at Hull House would easily have qualified for leadership in *any* women's movement. In an era when it was not often done, my colleagues Julia Lathrop and Mrs. Florence Kelley studied law and were admitted to the bar. Alice Hamilton was a physician, and a number of our other residents were women of distinguished accomplishment. I would be right at home with your aspiring women of today.

I do think that their work might profit from the introduction of a bit of humor though. I recall that nothing I wrote in support of women's suffrage was quite so effective as one piece in which I presented the state of affairs in an imaginary society where only women had the vote and men were agitating for the franchise. By turning all the arguments around with good humor, I think I was able to obtain more careful consideration of the state of affairs than were others of my day who were more angry in their mood.

It might come as a bit of a surprise to you, but I was really a latecomer to the suffrage movement. I believe I attended my first National American Woman Suffrage Association conference in 1906, which was the year Susan B. Anthony died. And of course she had first proposed a Constitutional amendment giving women the vote in 1869, almost 40 years before. It was only in the ten years before the Nineteenth Amendment was ratified that I became actively engaged in that important effort. So much of interest was going on even before the turn of the century; what a time *that* was for women!

To be sure, your own present time is also one of exciting and expanding possibilities for women. Indeed, I see many parallels when I consider the goals and efforts of your contemporary women's movements and those of my day. But you must realize how much more difficult the struggle was when we had presidents such as Harrison, Cleveland, and McKinley, when women who went to college were the exception, when there were a scant 38 million women in the nation and their average age was only 22. A woman of good sense who found herself committed to the ideal of equal political opportunity with men in 1800 was subject to considerable abuse. (I myself received more than one obscene letter in response to my work on behalf of the women's movement). The going seemed slow, I can tell you. Even as late as 1930, ten years after we began to vote, I wrote that "women in politics thus far have been too conventional, too afraid to differ with men, too unused to trust to their own judgment, too skeptical of the wisdom of the humble, to release the concern of simple women into the ordering of political life. . . . On the whole I am quite inclined to agree with Chesterton when he wrote, 'Many people have imagined that feminine politics would be merely pacifist or humanitarian or sentimental. The real danger of feminine politics is too much of a masculine policy' [1930a, p. 410]."

Why is it, do you think, that we seem to have produced no other Jane Addamses? With the possible exception of Eleanor Roosevelt, no other American woman has so totally dominated her age at home or abroad. Why not?

I would be flattered if I did not believe my prominence was as much a function of the particular times as of my own abilities. The world was simpler in many ways. As I mentioned before, there were fewer articulate and informed women in my day than now. And the causes I believed in struck at the hearts of more people. Many more people *personally* suffered from abuses of one sort or another: poverty, slum housing, industrial abuses. Reforms were so very evidently necessary. In that sense, I rode the crest of the times. And because the world was simpler and smaller, a few people could have broader impact than now.

I have always wondered too whether the nature of exposure to the media then and now contributes to the absence of heroes and heroines in your times. Nowadays, at the very least you have to be photogenic. In my day, in all the coverage of even the president, his family, his foibles, and his foolishness were treated more kindly, or not treated in the media at all. I wonder, for example, how well I would do for my causes today if NBC or CBS or ABC found my work, my writing, my speeches uninteresting—or worse, if they took a dislike to me. And today there is such competition for the philanthropic dollar and for publicity for one's cause. I do not envy the social work administrator of today who might wish to begin a new program or service. Even if he or she should be so fortunate as to gain a sound base, the moment the service grows to any size at all, there arise the problems a grant funding, state and federal accountability requirements, endless forms, and bureaucracies to which one must report. No, I am not at all sure the world would ever have heard of Jane Addams if she had done in 1975 only those good works she did in 1900.

Do you think, then, that any *social worker would have great difficulty in gaining recognition? I find it hard to believe that you would actually be obscure as a social worker in 1975.*

Social workers are perhaps inevitably doomed to obscurity. Just as society continues to sweep its social problems under the rug, so too it would just as soon sweep under the same rug those who choose to combat those social problems. We do not do popular work. We like to call ourselves The Conscience of Society, but we forget how ambivalent people usually are about their consciences. In 1930 I told the National Conference of Social Work that "it is perhaps all too customary for social workers to count up their achievements and to call upon the community for due appreciation. Such a custom has been in fact inherent in the situation itself, for while the doctor and the lawyer quietly and unobstrusively collect their fees from the individual upon whom their services have been bestowed, the social worker from necessity must collect his fees not from the people he has served whose pockets are perforce empty, but from the prosperous members of the community who are convinced that those services in the first place were necessary and in the second place have been well performed. Sometimes the social worker has to insist that the given services were both necessary to the social good and were well done in individual cases, against the very denials and shrill outcries of the recipients themselves . . . [1930b, p. 50]."

Do you think social workers ought to continue to serve in social programs when the recipients themselves cry out against the programs?

Well, you know, that very much depends on a variety of things. I think that one should look closely at services when recipients decry them, but I do not necessarily believe that such a fact alone means the service is inadequate. One has to look at all the data, evaluate carefully, and make up one's own mind about the value of the service—always considering, of course, what one takes to be the essential needs and nature of human behavior. Your question reminds me of one time when I was addressing a group of laborers, speaking out in strong support of some of their demands. One rough-looking man called out: "You are all right now, but, mark my words, when you are subsidized by the millionaires, you will be afraid to talk like this." I told the fellow that while I did not intend to be subsidized by millionaires, neither did I propose to be bullied by workingmen and that I should state my honest opinion without consulting either of them (1910, p. 185). We must use our own good brains to evaluate programs; neither the government, nor the funders, nor the recipients should hold full sway on what we think.

And it is that quality, the independence of mind, that really most distinguished our Hull House residents; that is why they were unique men and women. No one there was common; no one was typical. We had all come to that most precious discovery in human development: we each knew we were unlike any other human being, and each of us had a unique contribution to make. The variation from the established type is at the root of all change, the only possible basis for progress, all that keeps life from growing unprofitably stale and repetitious (1909, p. 21). That is why I so very much admired and respected Alice Hamilton and Julia Lathrop, Florence Kelley and Louise Bowen, Jessie Binford and the Brackenridge sisters: all of them had their own minds—independent, precise, critical—and all of them could speak their minds. They were among the reasons Hull House life was never stale.

And yet, however much you admired such colleagues as Alice Hamilton, Julia Lathrop, Florence Kelley, Louise Bowen, and the rest, whose names became part of social work history along with your own, you did not choose any of them as your closest confidant. Can you tell me a bit more about the woman who was your dearest friend, whose name is not at all known now, Mary Rozet Smith?

Mary Rozet Smith meant more to me than any other human in my life, save for my father. I first came to know her through her generous contributions to Hull House. But later in our lives, we vacationed together, traveled together, wrote each other daily when we were apart. Mary just came to devote herself to me, and there was nothing for it but to love her in return. She nursed me when I was sick, she purchased clothes for me, frequently paid my travel expenses: in short, she *cared* for me as no other did. Ours was not so much a meeting of minds, although Mary was interested in my work and gave time and energy to our programs, but far more than that. Ours was a meeting of the spirits.

All of us need love and concern, and throughout my life after I first met Mary in the 1890s, she was the one person with whom I most shared love and concern. When she died in 1934, I was cast into a depression as deep as when my father died. There can be little doubt that Mary mothered me; her maternal instinct toward me and her tender care of me were remarkable. It was something I admired in her perhaps even more than I admired intellect in others.

You once wrote that "the maternal instinct and family affection is woman's most holy attribute [Johnson, 1960, p. 201]."

Yes. And I still believe it. We have found no method superior to that of a loving mother for raising children to be sensitive, loving, secure individuals. Women, one by one, are better at child rearing and stabilization of society than any other factor we can name.

Yet Margaret Mead says that new family forms are emerging and society's base will be radically altered as the conventional family structure fades.

Well, you must remember that I am old fashioned; but I don't see it coming for a long while, at least not for the family of the common man. You see, you still have a massive problem with poverty in the United States and certainly worldwide as well. I am willing to grant the theoretical possibility of new forms of marriage and family life. But in present fact, many such new forms are based on abstract principles and ideals cultivated by the privileged or their offspring. I think perhaps the masses of men and women are still too insecure to experiment. The poor girl without skills in a weak economy will still cling to traditional family roles as security for herself and her children. And in her frustration and the difficulty of her life, she will raise her children to the same insecurities. And thus the wheel begins another turn. I saw it again and again in my Hull House neighborhood.

Now if society were really to move dramatically—to make the poor more secure economically, to train each to a skill, male *and* female, and then to provide an outlet for that skill—then perhaps in a few generations you might find genuine change in the traditional family forms. But I think those forms may prove markedly resistant to change, worldwide, until society permits each and every individual to succeed independently and with equality. And societies do not now do so.

Have you a word about unions? In your day, you were one of the most vocal and literate supporters of the unions in the world.

Yes. At that time they were the only ones doing what the whole of society ought to have been doing. But that is no longer true. No, I do not see *any* social institution acting on behalf of those in poverty, ill health, ignorance, or insecurity in the manner which unions used to do. Sadly, not even the social workers, who seem too busy with their internecine wars.

Knowing that very early in your work at Hull House, you entered the political arena to work against the corrupt alderman from your ward. . . .

Yes, we fought him, and lost.

I wonder what you think of our current political system and the crisis of confidence we have recently sustained?

I had certainly hoped for better once women got the vote! You know, though, even in 1898 I had some ideas about political machinations which seem relevant to your Watergate affair. I noted at that time, sadly, that "the successful candidate must not attempt to hold up a morality beyond . . . [that of his constituents], nor must he attempt to reform or change the standard. His safety lies in doing on a large scale what good deeds his constituents are able to do only on a small scale. If he believes what they believe, and does what they are all cherishing a secret ambition to do, he will dazzle them by his success and win their confidence [1898, p. 285]." Things seem not to have changed. It seems to me, therefore, that you might look to your politicians as a reflection of yourselves.

You learned your politics at the ward level, and later as a confidant of famous politicians, even presidents; you were active in one presidential campaign yourself even before you had the vote. You must know politics intimately. What advice would you have for us in the midst of our own political difficulties?

I have always said that I have so few answers! But I will say that you might try holding to an ideal, an hypothesis. You might demand a moral base from your politicians. I know that is an old-fashioned term and idea. It is true that high standards make the general company of men and women nervous. And, too, one must face the fact that ideas change less rapidly than events, so that much political thought is out of date and inappropriate to changed conditions.

But granting that, Americans have not served humanistic ideals well of late, if indeed they ever have. We are instead exceptional pragmatists, businessmen, and compromisers. We have produced few great philosophers, though many great tinkerers. Perhaps that is why, in part, social work remains a profession of relatively low status and why the other humanistic professions are under attack as well. Americans are suspicious of people who say they want to help or serve.

What remedy? I don't know. Perhaps each voter should scrutinize the character of those who seek office rather than scrutinize their policies. After all, policies arise from the nature and character of the policy-maker. Given my choice between a pessimist and an optimist, I should always vote for the optimist. Given a choice between one who in suffering had chosen symptoms of depression and another who acts out, I should always vote for the depressed one: he has struggled inwardly and may have profited, but the one who visits his suffering on others outside himself rarely has much feeling for his fellow man.

It might be of some value too to focus your attention on broader issues. What kind of society does permit the fullest growth of personality and the greatest economic and personal security for citizens? The society that gives whole-somely to its citizens, it seems to me, will find its citizens more able to give back.

In this view, I think perhaps I differ with your contem-porary conservatives, who seem to feel that the assistance of the broader society in meeting the social and economic needs of families inevitably undermines the family in its capacity to ultimately give back to the society. I feel it girds and strengthens them to do so. I suppose it can be true, for some, that suffering and travail are ennobling. But I sus-pect their numbers are few and that they are marked by their early griefs, even if triumphant over them. For most of us, it seems to me, the greater the social and economic ease, the more likely that the character will flower in a manner that will return benefit to society.

Are you saying that one need not suffer to help?

Certainly not in the sense of having to exactly dupli-cate in one's own life another's grief before helping. More-over, I found that a helping relationship need not be class conscious, which is an excellent thing since class differ-ences are now perhaps more striking than ever before. Class and status have no existence here in heaven, you know. They exist on earth, of course, but certainly they should not be vested with their past and present impor-tance. I crossed class lines to help—my whole life is a testi-mony to that—and others do so all the time. Of course it can be done.

You mention heaven. All your life you refused to speculate or make up your mind as to what you thought might follow death. What can you tell us about it?

Heaven is understanding what happened and what is now happening in the world and in the affairs of men. Now

I see clearly. Purgatory, on the other hand, which we must all pass through, who come here to heaven, is that one terrible moment when you see at last precisely why you did all that you did in life.

Terrible moment? But your life was one of exceptional accomplishment!

I think perhaps you misunderstood. I say, one sees then, not merely *what* one did, but also *why*. That is a revelation indeed.

REFERENCES

Addams, J. Ethical survivals in municipal corruption. *International Journal of Ethics,* April 1898, 273–279.

Addams, J. *The spirit of youth and the city streets.* New York: Macmillan, 1909.

Addams, J. *Twenty years at Hull House.* New York: Macmillan, 1910.

Addams, J. Aspects of the woman's movement. *Survey,* Aug. 1, 1930, 384–410. (a)

Addams, J. *The second twenty years at Hull House.* New York: Macmillan, 1930. (b)

Johnson, E. C. (Ed.) *Jane Addams, A centennial reader.* New York: Macmillan & Co., 1960.

Lasch, C. *The new radicalism in America, 1889–1963.* New York: Knopf, 1965.

YONATA FELDMAN has been for many years with the Jewish Board of Guardians in New York and on the faculty of Smith College School of Social Work.

Chapter 3

YONATA FELDMAN

I'll tell you a little bit about my life. I was born in Latvia, but very soon my family decided to move to Jurgev. That was a university town; it is in Estonia. Now, at that time Estonia was part of Imperial Russia. We moved there because it was a university town and to give the children an opportunity to go to school. I was of preschool age. I must have been three or four most likely because my little brother was already born. But the story starts when we first arrived. This I remember, we went to stay with an aunt, and my grandmother was there, and I was to sleep with my grandmother, which I very much disliked. And I said, "With an old lady I do not like to sleep!"

Well, we lived in that town for quite a while, and that's where I got my schooling. My beginning school years were very difficult. The first time, when my sister took me to school, the teacher called on me and I was so frightened I crawled under the desk! I would have surely been referred to the Jewish Board of Guardians if there were one. But with the Grace of God, I survived.

How many siblings did you have?

We were eight children. I came from a large, poor family. I was next to the youngest. My oldest sister was much older than I; she went to South Africa and she married there, so I didn't know her very well.

Well, anyway. I stayed a long time in school in Estonia. After that little school, I began to take private lessons. That was a little "folk" school and it had only a few grades. Later, I was one of the chosen ones of the family, because we were very poor and the other children went to work and whatever education they got, they got on their own. But my mother decided that I had to go to the gymnasium, which is the equivalent here of grammar school plus high school, and she hired a tutor to prepare me for entrance into the gymnasium. Actually, I enjoyed taking these private lessons because I took them from a medical student and he was an intriguing teacher. He really made learning extremely interesting.

When it was decided that I should go to the gymnasium, there was a law in Russia that 100 non-Jewish children were to be admitted to the school, then three Jewish children could be admitted. Now the Jewish children had to be admitted according to who was the highest academically—who passed the highest on an entrance examination. So, three times I took that examination! The third time I passed high enough and I was admitted.

Beginning school was very difficult for me because I wasn't disciplined when I came to school. I was rather tomboyish and I slid down the stairways, and what do you know, I landed in the lap of the principal of the school and was severely reprimanded!

Were you a good student?

No. Not in the beginning. However, learning has always been very intriguing to me, and I had all kinds of fantasies. Geography was the most fascinating subject for me—all about the world. As soon as I learned a few things,

I gathered all the children I knew and made a school, and everything I learned I taught them. I was a big performer, you know. It's very interesting, now that I think about it, that somehow the principal of the school very early started to tell me to help the other children to prepare their lessons. In fact, she gave me a salary.

A paraprofessional?

Yes, a paraprofessional. And not only that, but she herself had a daughter in my grade, so she invited me to prepare my lessons together with her. It was because she was a little duller than I that she wanted that. But then she started to give me other children to teach, even though I was not in a top grade.

Well, then I did take a course to be a teacher. They had a program that after having completed the gymnasium, there was an additional year you could take to prepare to be a teacher.

A Normal School?

Yes, like a Normal School. And then I taught school after graduation. I taught for quite a number of years.

I really enjoyed that school, and as years went by I enjoyed it more and more. The Russian inspector of schools came once, and after watching my lesson he said, "If you were not Jewish, I would have you come and teach other teachers how to teach." He came to a lesson in arithmetic and we had a great deal of fun in that arithmetic lesson, so he was very much impressed. So you see that very early I really was a good teacher. The principal of our gymnasium. . . .

The one that you ran into from the bannister?

Yes. She was very friendly with the director of the university and it was a famous university: the Imperial University of Jurgev. Russia had seven universities in all, and this was an outstanding one. The director decided that he would open higher education for women, and the principal suggested that I take these courses. So I did, and there I studied history and philology. After a while, the thing didn't work out financially, but the director had tremendous political pull, so by special permission from the government, he got all the women (and we were a small crowd of about 40) into the university. So we became the first women in the university.

Did you complete your university training there?

No, I did not complete it; you see the First World War broke out. Well anyway, the way I got here is that the Joint Distribution Committee [an international Jewish relief and refugee organization] came to Estonia and one member of the committee, when he found out that I had relatives in Chicago, was able to get me a visa and helped me to emigrate.

Did you want to leave?

Yes. I wanted to leave because there was nothing I could do in Estonia. There was no way for me to advance, and I had relatives here. Actually, I wanted to go to Israel, but I didn't have any relatives in Israel and I didn't have money.

In those days, it was Palestine?

Palestine, yes. I have always been a Zionist. So actually I went to Chicago, where I had two uncles and a sister. I stayed with my sister.

Did you teach there?

No. First I went to preparatory school to learn the language, and then I got several jobs. It was very funny about my jobs. I didn't know the language, and my first job was in a bank where I was supposed to answer the telephone. Because the Joint Distribution Committee member was a judge in Chicago, he was able to get me the job. Out of respect for him and perhaps for political reasons, they would have kept me, but I was supposed to answer telephones and for me it was just awful—I could not understand a word of the message. I felt foolish so I resigned. They must have been grateful because they gave me a week's wages. Then my next job was addressing envelopes. I spoiled a thousand envelopes because I didn't know the streets and they were hand written and I copied them all wrong. Well I also quit that job in two days. They were also glad to get rid of me. Finally, I landed a job in an orphan asylum, and there I really learned how to speak English. Because of the children, you see—I had to speak to the children in nothing but English. The children were lovely and they were very patient teachers. You would think that they would make fun of me? No.

You were an orphan too in a way.

I was an orphan too and they must have felt it. And I felt for them because they were really miserably treated in the orphan asylum.

Who ran the orphan asylum?

It was a Jewish organization. But the head of the board of directors was a brother-in-law of one of the richest Jews. And don't you see, this was why he had the job, not because he was fit to run it.

What were your duties? Were you a child care worker?

Yes. A child care worker, but I didn't stay there long. I decided to see if I could get into the university because I had gotten a job in a smaller institution, the Ruth Club for Girls. A number of older girls there had started college at the University of Chicago. Because the Ruth Club was geographically close to that university, I decided to see if I could finish my studies there. To my great sorrow, they gave me credit for a bachelor's degree and I started graduate work without knowing the language well—just on my marks. You see, I didn't have any certificate to show because when the Germans were in Estonia they looted the university. I thought I couldn't get my papers to show that I had had a course in comparative languages given by an Estonian, Professor Masing. That course in comparative languages ran for four years. Well, I found him and asked him if there were any records left. He was sick at that time, but he had a book where the marks were put in—how long the course lasted and the marks. Now, at the university all my marks were excellent, for the simple reason that the system was not like here. You take a course there and whenever you're ready to pass the examination, you call up the professor and you go to his office and take the test. Well, I just wouldn't go until I knew the subject thoroughly, and therefore I had all very good marks.

I know now that what I studied was certainly equivalent to a bachelor's degree, but at that time I didn't know English well enough for graduate study. I knew Russian and German, and when I came to Professor Albion Small, who was the dean of the Sociology Department and the father of sociology in the United States (a very educated man who had studied in Germany), I spoke to him in German. He gave me the equivalent of a bachelor's degree. I told him that I worked part-time with children, and he started me in the Sociology Department with three graduate courses plus one undergraduate course. One course was with Dr. Small, "Philosophy of History," and, though advanced, it was very easy for me because it had a rich German bibliography.

I also studied anthropology with Dr. Frazier, a very fine professor. I came in and, do you know, I cannot understand a word he's saying! How I ever finished I can't understand because I had to look up every word in the dictionary.

My first years at the university were most difficult. First of all, in the Ruth Club where I worked, the superintendent got sick and I took her place, since I was her assistant. Before she left to go to the hospital, she told me that it was very easy to run the place. She said she had a cook who was very good and a maid and janitor. They would give me a list of what I had to order in the grocery or somewhere else and I just had to telephone. On this I depended. In the morning, when the children went to school, I rushed to take my courses at the University of Chicago. Once the janitor gave me a list of things to order. So during the intermission between two courses, I look at the list and I see all kinds of things. Everything has a pound, you know—three pounds, six pounds. Only one item has no pounds, so I thought I'd ask for five pounds or six pounds. A wheelbarrow. I said "A five-pound wheelbarrow." So they said "What! We haven't got a five-pound wheelbarrow." I immediately rushed to the dictionary. Well, I'll tell you. When I saw the janitor, I said "How come you tell me to order a wheelbarrow in the grocery?" This colored man started to laugh, and, from then on, whenever he saw me he burst into terrific laughter.

Well, after a year in sociology, I really learned the language, and I also learned how to get around the university—how to use the different resources, the library, for instance. I had a terrible time using the library. I thought that it was like in Russia where, when we were given a reference, it meant you had to study the book from beginning to end. I asked for the book and they said E 11. Now someone, Mr. E 11, has the book, I thought. So I came a little later and asked for the book and they again said E 11. I couldn't understand why the library permitted one person to keep a book so long. Finally, I found a student who had enough patience to listen to me. When I explained to him about Mr. E 11, he said: "You're a goose. E 11 is a room, Room E on the 11th floor and all your reference books for the course are there." Well, he did me a great favor because from then on I could use the library.

After a year I decided that there was no reason for me to study sociology because I wouldn't be able to teach because of my language difficulties. I felt that social work was really the profession I wanted, and so I transferred to the Department of Social Service. And of course social work was much, much easier for me because by now I knew the language well enough and, in addition, the faculty took a personal interest in me, and by the Grace of God, I graduated and got my master's degree. Do you know that at that time Chicago was giving social workers a doctor's degree? The university strongly urged me to remain and get a doctor's degree. However, I couldn't afford it. Besides, I was so tired of studying.

Did you remain at the orphanage?

No. I quit that institution. I quit a year before because I had to devote much more time to my studies.

During that time you were living with your sister?

Yes. I couldn't have done this without her. She supported me. In the second year, I got a fellowship in the school of social work. I paid for one semester, but the next semester I really couldn't afford to go through so they gave me a fellowship.

When I got the fellowship, it meant that I worked with Miss Edith Abbott. Miss Abbott was writing a book on immigration and she used me to translate letters of immigrants. I was proud and happy to work with Miss Abbott because I admired her as a teacher and a person.

My first placement was with a non-Jewish family agency, and it was in a neighborhood where there were Czechoslovakian people, German people, and Polish people. When I came to the agency, the social worker who was supervising me couldn't speak to any of the people. Therefore, she had a great deal of trouble because the children had to translate. But I knew German, and since in Russia I was learning the Slavic languages as part of my university studies in philology, I could read and I could also speak a little. So the agency assigned me cases where I could utilize my knowledge. They had a German family whom they supported—a large German family—but they couldn't speak with them. When I came and I spoke German, this woman told me that her husband's father went to America very early, but she doesn't know where he is. Finally, she produced a letter that his father sent them a long time ago when they were still overseas. I looked at that letter and I see that the father tells them that he has worked in Indiana in one of the steel mills. What do you know, I get myself busy, take a train, go out to Indiana, and fish up the old man. Oh God! Do you know how happy that man was? He was ready to support his grandchildren.

Another one was a Czechoslovakian family. The father had tuberculosis and since it was infectious, by law he was placed in an institution. He didn't know why he was placed in an institution.

You mean no one explained the nature of the illness?

Apparently not, so every once in a while he'd run away and his wife would hide him. The authorities wanted her to bring the children for a medical examination. She absolutely refused. She locked the door and they had terrific trouble. They just couldn't manage the whole thing. Well, they gave me these wonderful cases—the cases they couldn't manage. I went there and do you know how happy that woman was when I started to speak with her in a few words of Czechoslovakian? With my Russian and Czechoslovakian, I was able to explain to her that he was sick and they don't want the children to become infected—that in fact they want to prevent the children from getting sick. She brought them in for a medical examination.

But then your own experiences in social work shifted because, when you started, "environmental manipulation" were certainly not dirty words.

But let me tell you that Dr. Sheldon Gluck, the psychiatrist and psychoanalyst from Boston, came to Chicago. He gave us ten lectures on Freud. Not only did the faculty think this stuff was crazy, we thought Freudians were awful people, myself included. Because it was crazy. Who has sexual feeling toward your own father? Absolutely crazy. And so we rejected the Freudian theory. All the students were very upset. They thought it was scandalous and so did our faculty and therefore. . . . We were environmental people, you see.

So when did you decide that Freud was not scandalous?

I'll tell you. When I started to work, I first applied to the Jewish Family Service in Chicago. The director rejected me. He said, "We can't have you because you don't know American life." But I said, "I know Jewish life." He said "We're not interested in Jewish life and Jewish customs."

Who was he; do you remember?

Sure. Karp, the director of the School of Social Work. You remember there was a school of social work here in New York. It was a special school that the Jews opened. You see, this was the joke—that he said Jewish culture is not important.

Jews have that problem.

Yes. Jews have that problem. But I did get a job in a placement agency. And there I worked with children because I had been a school teacher and children ate out of the palm of my hand.

This was a foster care agency?

Yes. They realized my particular ability with difficult children, and they had me take courses with the Institute of Juvenile Research. There I learned psychiatric social work and began learning from the children I was working with. The children taught me that Freud was right.

I see. So you didn't think he was so crazy?

No. And when I started working at the Jewish Board of Guardians, I found that his theories made more and more sense.

How did you get to the Jewish Board of Guardians?

I got to the Jewish Board of Guardians because I married a man who wanted to move to New York. I met him in Chicago. He was a University of Chicago student. My husband got a Ph.D. in chemistry first, and then he got a degree in medicine at Rush Medical College, but he never practiced in Chicago. He started practicing here in New

York, where we married. I came to New York, and then I
got this job at the Jewish Board of Guardians.

*Then this was your only professional life in New York—with
the Jewish Board of Guardians?*

I never worked in any other organization in New York.
So I really have only worked with two agencies: the Jewish
Homefinding Society in Chicago and the Jewish Board of
Guardians in New York.

The Jewish Board of Guardians at that time was a most
disorganized place. In fact, for a long time I didn't know
what I was supposed to do there because they had all kinds
of divisions—they worked with unmarried mothers, they
worked with prisoners. We were the probation officers for
all the Jewish prisoners, and everybody worked in one
room. There were all kinds of things going on.

Mr. Sievers was the director, and also, at that time, the
Jewish Board of Guardians had the members of the board
constantly around. Many of them would tell the social
workers what to do, and they sat in on psychological conferences. They were constantly in and out.

*That board of directors, as you describe it, sounds a lot like the
way you talk about your early years in social work. Then too, the
social workers like Mary Richmond and Jane Addams were also very
involved, in the pre-Freudian sense.*

Of course. I couldn't even imagine anything but working with the environment.

And yet you changed as the movement changed?

I changed, but I didn't give up; I still don't give up on
the environment. It's a very important factor. What happened to me was that I integrated the mental unconscious
forces with the environment, considering the mental forces
equal if not dominant over the environment, because now
I understand that people change the environment and that
the environment is people. People make the environment,
and their understanding and their emotional conditions

can change it. Therefore I think the study of sociology and anthropology helped me a great deal.

Because it gave a theoretical basis to your later actual work in the environment?

Absolutely.

But you made a shift when you embraced Freudian psychology?

That's correct. Because my work with people convinced me that the environment is not all.

Well, when you worked in your first field placement with the Czechoslovakian lady and explained her husband's illness, you certainly manipulated the environment.

No. I didn't with that Czechoslovakian woman. I did not change anything in her environment. You know what I changed? I changed her understanding that her husband was not being abducted. And the reason is because I could communicate with her. I became a human being speaking to a human being. Now, what the others did was manipulate her environment in order to help her. That means they removed her husband who could infect her and the children with tuberculosis.

What about when you went to Indiana, when you were working with the lady who showed you the letter?

Why did she show *me* the letter and not the other social worker? Because she couldn't talk to her. She was a stranger who only gave her bread, yes? But she had no human relationship with that social worker.

Do you think that was only because you knew something of the language? Would it have been possible for someone else, who didn't know the language to have gotten that letter?

No. Because you have to ask the children to translate. Then you don't know what the children tell the mother, do you? There is no communication. With me there was communication. She did not think to remember the letter; only when she could tell me her life story could I ask if she did not have a letter from her father-in-law.

So with you there was a possibility of a relationship.

Suddenly she found that we were not just the givers of bread. Here was a woman to whom she could describe her emotional needs. That she was left alone with children. That her husband had died. That she was in a strange country. That she didn't know what to do. That she hasn't got anyone close to her. But as soon as a woman comes who can speak her language, she already feels close.

Once I saw a woman—a Russian woman—in Chicago. She couldn't speak English. When I started to speak to her in Russian, she said, "Oh, finally I meet a relative." I'm not her relative. But as long as she felt she could tell me how she felt—that she felt lost, she didn't know where to go—then she felt she was with a relative.

Well, what is the therapeutic relationship? The therapeutic relationship requires that your client or patient, whatever you call him, suddenly feels understood. It is a mother who understands the needs of a child that creates a therapeutic relationship. Then your client becomes an understood child because he's in need and you understand him. Therefore, you can help him. In this sense, that Russian woman was a lost child and I was her mother. I was going to show her how to get where she wanted to go.

Do you think that when you immigrated and you struggled yourself that you were a lost child?

Absolutely. In the orphan asylum, I was an orphan and my orphan children sensed it.

In a way, you combined your teaching and then your feelings of being lost and an orphan in your work with the emotionally disturbed. It must have been very chaotic to be in a new country with no knowledge of the language. So you must have understood the unconscious chaos of these children.

Yes. When I came to the University of Chicago, the elevator man was a Russian who was stranded here. As soon as he learned I was from Russia, he took the greatest interest in me. He introduced me to all the professors. And he would say, "This is my landlady." You see, he felt close to me, and I was happy to know him. I felt at home because of that man, because he spoke Russian.

He was not a Jew, he was a Russian. He felt this country was a most beautiful country because Miss Abbott took a personal interest in him. She went with him and got him citizenship papers, and she was extremely kind to him. And he said that in Russia, a professor would never take such an interest in a plain man. He was one of the people at the University of Chicago who made me appreciate this country.

Good social work was always social work that took into consideration human feelings.

Do you think that's still taught and practiced?

I hope it is. I know it's practiced by the best social workers; let's put it that way. And therefore I welcome the clinical social workers' organization because they represent social workers who want to work with people. They want to integrate our inner and outer needs and they didn't go back and say we have to improve the environment. They know they have to work with people and with their emotions, and this is why I'm very much for the clinical social workers. They have their hearts in the right place.

You are still a consultant to the Jewish Board of Guardians?

Of course, but in a very limited way now.

How may years did you spend there?

Enough. I came there in 1928.

You were with the Jewish Board of Guardians in the days when it was Rankian?

Of course. When Dr. John Slawson became the director, he hired Elizabeth Dexter. Now Miss Dexter was a Rankian—a beautiful woman and a Rankian, a trained social worker.

What did you get from the exposure to Rankian theory?

I got a lot from the Rankians, particularly the skill of interviewing. I think, in the skill of interviewing, the Rankian school was superior. I have to tell you a funny story. Rank was here in New York and gave a course—ten lectures —and I attended it. Now, you know Rank disclaimed that what the social workers were doing here was his theory. They continuously kept asking him questions, and then when he would answer them as to how a situation should be treated, they would say, "But Dr. Rank, you don't know America." So finally he said to them, "You are coming to listen to my theory. If you want to know my theory, ask me something I know and don't tell me I don't know America." You see, they were giving him their theory, which he disclaimed.

So he was saying, "You don't know Rankian theory."

That's correct. He was saying, "Don't tell me this is my theory. If you want to know my theory, please listen to me."

How do you account for that?

Because they modified Rankian theory to suit their own ideas. And I'm sorry to say that their ideas did not always make sense. But they knew interviewing skills well. I think that they had better ideas about transference—what goes on in the interview, what goes on right between the worker and the client—but they surrounded it with a lot of ideas that didn't make sense to me. That was not Rank's theory at all.

When did you meet Dr. Paul Federn? I know he had a great influence in your work.

Ah, yes, Dr. Federn: a fine gentleman. I supervised someone in a reading group he led (Mrs. Betty Gabriel), and I was invited to it. The reading group only consisted of people who were analyzed, and at that time I was not yet analyzed. Now, of course, I was very flattered. From then on he really took a very great interest in me, and I benefited by my contact with him through this group. We were all social workers and Dr. Federn led us in reading Freud, except he was not only explaining Freud but he was also giving us his own contributions to the understanding of the ego.

He was a psychiatrist, and he was from where?

Oh, he was a pupil of Freud's, but he worked with psychotics. He was a Viennese himself. He always said that social workers are more capable, because of their training, to handle psychotic people than psychiatrists are. He was referring to the fact that a psychotic needs a continuous and constant contact which psychiatrists usually cannot afford to give and that they also need environmental support. In fact, he thought that every psychotic should have two analysts so that when he develops paranoid ideas about one he can go to the other.

Was he, would you say, one of the greatest influences on your professional life?

No, I wouldn't say that, but he was a great influence. The greatest was Dr. van Opuijsen. He was a wonderful teacher. He was a better teacher than Federn. To me, Federn was a very great supportive influence.

However, the most profound contribution to my present day understanding and treatment of clients was made by Dr. Hyman Spotnitz. I do not think that Dr. van Opuijsen or our other consulting psychiatrists were fully aware of how many of our clients—children as well as their parents—were really borderline psychotics. If the symptoms were acute, it was suggested to us that we refer such a client—parent or child—to an outpatient service of a mental hospital. When I followed up these cases, I learned that they never even applied. No wonder, they feared of being committed! We social workers, who knew that mental hospitals could offer no help to these clients, were reluctant to carry out such a psychiatric recommendation; we would be particularly against committing a child.

At times, some of our consulting psychiatrists would feel that though our client was psychotic and beyond help, he or she was still in need of some human contact and would refer the case to us for supportive treatment.

Then some of us started to experiment to treat border-line psychotic clients, children, and their parents. We were asked to choose a client that we thought could be helped. We worked with Dr. Spotnitz and from him learned how important it is to approach a person who is in depression and despair with a feeling of hopefulness. It was an exciting experience for me and my co-workers to carry cases under intensive and continuous supervision, individually and in a group. As we understood the magnitude of the infantile rage our clients had to cover up by withdrawal, by acting out, and by physical illness in order to survive, and as we ourselves were enabled to tolerate rage and many other things, we were astonished to see some fundamental improvements in our clients.

Was Dr. van Opuijsen's specialty working with children?

No, not at all. He only learned about children when he came to the Jewish Board of Guardians. And I must tell you that when he came to the Jewish Board of Guardians, he spent about three months doing nothing but reading cases. And after he would study a person's case, he would call us in and say: "Now why did you do that? I don't know your discipline, but I just want to know why you did it." Do you see he was studying social work deeply before he figured out what he had to teach us and how to teach it so that we could apply whatever he had to give, and in that respect he was a superior teacher. And do you know what happened? I was so impressed with Dr. van Opuijsen's ideas that I'd often say to him, "Dr. van Opuijsen, why don't you write it up?" And he said, "Oh, I don't like to write," or something like that.

Then I was asked to teach mental hygiene problems of children at the New York School. Well, naturally, I took the reading list, and though I had read very many of the books,

I decided, before I started teaching the course, I had to read the darn things over again, and many of them were my own books that I had bought. Can you imagine my surprise when I started rereading the books and found that many of the things that Dr. van Opuijsen taught me were right in the books. It wasn't anything new. It took me years of practice before I integrated the ideas that were Freud's ideas, not van Opuijsen's, but I didn't understand that then. The experience helped me a great deal in teaching because I knew that it is one thing to teach and another thing to integrate. Integration is difficult because you have to adjust your own psychic life in order to accept difficult and sometimes disturbing ideas.

At Smith College I was teaching the advanced students, the ones that were getting their doctor's degree. I was teaching them supervision and they brought in their own cases. When I started discussing the cases with them, it seemed they had never heard about a lot of the concepts I brought out to them. So I thought: By golly, who in heaven teaches them casework? I didn't express my idea, not wanting to insult my colleagues, but if they had had a course in advanced casework, how come they didn't know concepts that were so simple? They should know them. Well, one nice day, to my great regret, I taught both. They asked me to teach the first course. I taught the same group the first year advanced casework course, and I thought I was doing a lovely job, and then I taught them supervision the second year. Well, when I repeated the same concepts I taught them the previous year, they said, "Mrs. Feldman, how come you didn't tell us that last year?" And then I knew. I told them that last year they didn't hear it; they hadn't integrated it. You see, it takes time to fully understand and absorb a concept—it needs supervised experience.

And yet in a way social work education strives for just that in the way it relates practice and theory.

That's right.

Did van Opuijsen influence you because you were ready to integrate then?

Yes. And because he was a patient person.

So it was a combination of his personality and your time of life, so to speak.

And also his ability to teach. He was a great teacher. Some teachers are better able to help you integrate. I mean that a teacher who knows how difficult it is to integrate the concept would make it easier for a person to integrate it.

What you're saying would be not very modern in terms of today's view toward paraprofessionals and reducing professional standards. I assume you would take a dim view of people who have not had fairly extensive training because, when you talk about integration, you are talking about a whole learning experience.

Yes. That has to be slow.

That goes beyond acquisition of knowledge. It has to do with digestion of knowledge too.

That's right, and I think learning has to be slow because of this. Some people think that if a person goes to a school of social work, he doesn't need further supervision. No, I think that a school of social work doesn't allow for enough time, even with the best training, to integrate the concepts learned in school. And yet I think it is *most* important that social workers should be able to integrate intellectual concepts into work.

So what you're saying is that schools of social work should have more post-masters programs.

Yes, if social workers don't get such training in the agencies. Social work school is only a beginning by its very nature because students don't even get the whole process of training. They get only the honeymoon of a relationship, the beginning, but the trouble only starts after—in the working through. My idea is that social workers have to have the same training as an analyst now because they get the same problems. It seems to me that you have to adjust yourself to the needs of what you're doing. If you're a social worker in an agency and you really want to help this woman resolve a marital problem or be able to bring up children, and if she has a depression, you're not going to treat her by paying her rent. You have to have the skills to resolve her depression. And if she has a narcissistic disorder, you're not going to help her child. Therefore, if you're only paying the rent, you're just kidding yourself. You are not helping her.

Do you see social work moving in that direction?

Until recently I didn't. I thought it was moving exactly in the opposite direction. But now with the clinical social workers appearing, I hope that the schools of social work will understand these needs and give the proper training.

Do you know how long social work agencies felt that only a psychiatrist could treat a child?

A long time.

For me, treating children and working with children was the fundamental impetus for accepting psychoanalytic theory.

Anna Freud has said that the training of all analysts should include at least one case of child analysis.

Absolutely. Treating children should be a prerequisite for every social worker and every analyst. Particularly those who treat narcissistic disorders have got to have a deep understanding of the treatment of children.

One final thing. My own experience in the Bronx office of the Jewish Board of Guardians was certainly a highlight of my own professional development, and I'm very grateful for the training that I got there. The Bronx office was a very special place, I think, because you allowed everyone there to develop in their own way. You let people do their thing before it was popular.

Yes. I believe that's the way to do it.

I think you're right—I know it certainly was true with me— but how did you come to understand that? You developed a tremen-

*dously creative atmosphere, an atmosphere where many good thera-
pists developed.*

What is a creative attitude? Isn't a creative attitude
something very individual, something that should be different from anybody else's?

Yes. But you tolerated that.

Well, that's why I tolerated it.

*But how? So many people cannot do that. What helped you to
do it?*

Because I think what you learn by yourself you know
100 percent better than what you are taught by somebody.
Sometimes workers would come to me and say I want to do
this and this. I would say, "Well, the other thing seems
better." Then they would say, "No, I think this is," and I
would let them go ahead, even though I knew it was a
mistake.

Even if they lost the case?

Yes, even if they lost the case, because I think it is
better for them to lose the case and learn a lesson and
therefore treat 100 other cases better. And if they lose the
case there is no harm because people come back if they
have trouble.

There is a difference between consultation and training. In consultation you address yourself to what is best for
the client. Therefore, when I supervise in training I don't
supervise the case, I supervise the worker. I study the
worker, not the record, and how I can supervise her better.
If workers feel that their way is the best way, I let them try
it. I think it's much better that they try and lose the case
rather than not learn casework. Don't you think so?

*Yes, I think so, if I were losing the case under your supervision.
I don't know how I would feel about it if I were losing the case from
someone who would have nothing to teach me.*

I think it is very kind of you to be so complimentary of
me, but you are neglecting to mention that no other organ-

ization could have provided me with the intellectual stimulation that the Jewish Board of Guardians did—and also the freedom that permitted experimentation and growth. The administration encouraged the development of new and interesting ideas.

As far as professional development is concerned, I think I am lucky I suffer from separation anxiety and therefore only worked for two agencies from 1923 until today.

Photo Credit: Walter H. Scott, Stockbridge, Mass.

FRITZ REDL was for twelve years Professor of Social Work at the School of Social Work, Wayne State University, Michigan. Two of his best known books (with David Wineman) are *Children Who Hate* (1951) and *Controls from Within* (1952).

Chapter 4

FRITZ REDL

If you had to pin a label on yourself, what would your professional label be?

I really don't like labels. I think they make things appear too simple; they cover up the complexity of things. But I did receive a Ph.D. in philosophy and psychology from the University of Vienna in 1925.

Did you work then as a psychologist?

No. I began my work as a secondary school teacher in Vienna. The Vienna Board of Education at that time was involved in a lot of reformations initiated by socialist-oriented groups. Among them was an attempt to make the school system a little less rigid and authoritarian. While this effort was primarily centered in the school reform movement of the grade school system, some of it also penetrated the high school system, even though that remained more formalized for a long time. Among those innovations, one I liked very much was a ruling that, once a month, every high school class had to be taken by their teacher on a trip into the lovely surroundings of Vienna, and in the winter we had a chance to take our whole class skiing for a week into the higher Alps. This was done to loosen up the rigidity of classroom teaching and get teacher and kids together in a much more informal and personal relationship. I found this opportunity especially welcome, and it was here that I became very much interested in the process of group psychology. I was, of course, also very much interested in child psychology and had been involved in training as a psychoanalyst at the Vienna Psychoanalytic Society. In fact, I was among the few educators who were allowed to start their training in child analysis before I had finished my adult control cases.

Why was there such a limitation?

At that time, child analysis was still a very young offspring of the psychoanalysis of adults, and Anna Freud had plenty of trouble to explain that this was still analysis, even though techniques and procedures seemed quite revolutionary for those who worked with adults. The difference of work with children was marked of course: no couch, no free association, actual play with the patients, and close contact with their families, etc., etc.—I am sure that if anybody but the "Pope's" own daughter had made such a suggestion, they would have been forced to call this anything but analysis!

Did you have to undergo analysis yourself?

Of course. Editha Sterba and, later, Lampl de Groot were my personal analysts. My adult controls were under the supervision of Heinz Hartmann and Herman Nunberg, and of course much of my training involved such persons as Anna Freud, August Aichorn, and Marianne Kris.

You were not an M.D., nor were some of the other child educators to be trained as child analysts. Why was that?

In Austria the relationship between child analysis and education was a close one. In fact, our training was meant to bring the two fields closer together. It was for this reason that people who were active as educators were especially selected for psychoanalytic training.

Did you know Maria Montessori?

Yes, I was involved with the Montessori movement. I knew Maria Montessori personally and lectured at the movement's conferences, though I was not a Montessori teacher.

What was your interest in the Montessori movement?

During the years after the rightist revolution against the socialists in Vienna, there was heavy pressure against any innovative move, including child analysis and more modern trends in early childhood education. Only Catholic orders could afford to continue their work undisturbed. Mussolini, whose power was behind much of the rightist government pressures, could not very well object since Maria Montessori was a Catholic. Consequently, some of the kindergardens and preschool centers of Vienna which were run by Catholic agencies became a sort of haven for any progressive work with children and remained relatively unmolested by political pressures.

When did you come to America?

In 1936. I was invited by the General Education Board of the Rockefeller Foundation to participate in a two-year study of normal adolescence. The person who really brought me here was Robert Havighurst; the study was under the leadership of Caroline Zachry and located at the Progressive Education Association in New York. I am sure you have, in the meantime, heard some of the other names of people involved in the same project: Erik Erikson, Peter Blos, George Sheviakov, to name just a few.

Of course, in 1938 I did not return to Vienna, as I was originally expected to do—a guy by the name of Adolph Hitler had taken over after I arrived here. There was one member of our project by the name of Lindquist, who was principal of one of the very advanced high schools in Columbus, Ohio. He had just been offered the job of headmaster of the Cranbrook School in Bloomfield Hills, Michigan—a very fancy boarding school on the outskirts of Detroit. He asked me to go with him and help him develop its Guidance Department, together with Harry Hoey. I lived at that school for two years, working there half-time and teaching half-time at the University of Michigan.

A few years later, I began to commute between Ann Arbor and Chicago, where Dan Prescott had developed another Rockefeller Foundation project for teacher education. Eventually, I landed at Wayne State University—in 1941—as professor of group work in the School of Public Affairs and Social Work.

At Wayne State, did you teach full-time in the School of Social Work?

Yes. And this is, by the way, very funny indeed, for I had no idea what I was getting into when I took that job.

Were you teaching courses in casework?

Yes. But then they wanted me to help build up their group work sequence. Now here is where the funny part comes in. I had been increasingly interested in group psychology and its clinical ramifications, so I thought this would be just what I was hoping to get into. In fact, I had just published my paper "Group Emotion and Leadership" in 1942 in *Psychiatry.* What I found I was supposed to develop, though, was something quite different. I soon learned what was wanted by the YM-YWCA, and especially the settlement movement, was all that goes into developing the then traditional group work skills.

At the same time, I was, of course, very much interested in the summer camp that the University of Michigan had near Ann Arbor. This seemed to me a most promising design, far beyond the original concept of fresh-air vacations for city kids; they used it as part of the training for their schools of education, psychology, and social work. These students got classes and seminars as well as field-work credit out of it.

After a while, I developed my own camp on a similar design. It was called Camp Chief Noonday. I named it after the Michigan recreation area where it was located and it was to extend its program to girls as well as boys. We got our kids from detention homes, reformatories, and from a variety of social agencies. As staff, we had people from different disciplines, and we had group workers learn something about group psychology. But that was a source of some trouble for awhile. At that time, the traditional group work field wasn't interested in things like group psychology—to say nothing about group therapy. The traditional representatives of the group work field were quite upset about me, for they thought that their students should only work with the normal and had no business to mess with the abnormal at all. Besides, I was a psychoanalyst by training, and God only knows what I might do to their students, making them work with crazy kids and so forth. However, they let me have people who became my best staff—like Mary Lee Nicholson, Selma Fraiberg, and many more.

In order to create a proper fieldwork experience for my students, I developed the Detroit Group Project and the Detroit Group Project Summer Camp. Both were sponsored by the Detroit Council of Social Agencies and some private foundations, and the university allowed me to use my time for it. I didn't want to call any of this group therapy at that time. We were not pretending to do group therapy. If group work and camping is a good thing, it should also be able to be modified to become a helpful commodity for work with disturbed youngsters. Of course, you have to work differently with kids who are disturbed or delinquent, but that doesn't necessarily make it therapy. However, even wanting them to have a good group experience, you have to adapt your program and style of handling kids considerably, just as you would have to adapt a diet for somebody who is sick, or feed somebody who can't swallow by getting food into him some other way for a while.

What did you call it?

I called it "clinical group experience"; "clinical" because it had to do with having respect for the basic disturbances and was not just an educational experience. I didn't want to call it therapy because there were many things that I just couldn't fix up in a summer. These kids had many problems, and I was not even pretending to resolve all of them. I wanted them to have as good a summer camp experience as a normal kid would get.

You were looking for a much broader experience for them, not just a therapeutic one.

Well, you see, the word therapeutic is used in many ways. Just because something's good for you doesn't mean it's therapeutic, and just because it's therapeutic doesn't mean you don't need something else.

So you were distinguishing between group therapy and a clinical group experience.

Yes. The children were referred by social agencies, so some of them had had casework, but they still needed a group experience. Not everything could be taken care of in casework. On the other hand, the group was not a substitute for casework. On the contrary, group work and casework are two different commodities which need to be combined for some kids. And I hesitated to call it group therapy because therapy smacks of too much pretentiousness; also, even if their basic neuroses were not cured during the summer, they still had a good camp experience.

You were ready, then, to accept a short-range goal for these kids in a summer camp.

But it gets complex now because I had two projects. I had groups all year round, and in summer we expanded into a camp. I had some of the youngsters in casework (a casework agency carried them) and I had them in my activity groups—therapy groups, if you want to call them that—my clinical groups.

And then in 1944 I started Pioneer House, which was a residential treatment home where a kid could be an inpatient for the rest of the year.

Were you familiar with Slavson's activity group therapy?

Yes. My quarrel with Slavson at that time was, first of all, I couldn't swallow his total permissiveness, which was absolute nonsense with the type of kids I had, and, second, I was bothered by some of his structuring. For his kids, it fit very well, but for kids from the slum areas of Detroit, it didn't fit at all. Our main population was the delinquent child.

I remember one incident when I went to see Slavson because I was interested in his book, which came out about that time. He was so sure of what group therapy was supposed to be, but our staff felt that in our case it wasn't quite the same; we couldn't be that permissive. So I had a long talk with him. He was very delightful, very pleasant, and we had a lot of communication—except that he never quite trusted me. He always referred to me as that sociologist from Cleveland. I never was in Cleveland, except for a short time, and I'm not a sociologist, I'm a psychoanalyst. When I talked with him, we had one special problem with our project at the time Selma Fraiberg was in charge. The problem was that we had told the kids that when they made something, they could take it home. But they would also take the hammers and saws home too. So how do we handle that? We weren't sure because we didn't want to be nonpermissive. On the other hand, we wanted the stuff back; the kids couldn't just take anything, and they got confused. So what Slavson said was: "Oh, this is very simple. I'll tell you what we do."

And I said, "What?"

"Well, the group leader would not say anything. I would not say anything. But I would write a letter to the group leader in which I make a point that things are disappearing and it's important that they not disappear, that they stay here. Then the group worker would leave the letter around on the table, then the kids would find it, would read it, and then would have a discussion around it."

Now, this is fine, but not with my kids. First of all, most of my kids can't read, and, second, if they found the letter they would say, "Stick it! What are you cluttering our place for? You taught us to clean up and you leave your letters around!"

It just doesn't work, you know, because for different kids you have to have different methods. It's as simple as that. So Slavson was a little bit upset because he thought we were competitive. But I didn't feel that way at all because I had a different bunch of youngsters.

At that time, I taught a class in a combination of group work and casework techniques; that's the first thing I did at Wayne. I felt that group workers didn't really know or get enough experience in interview technique, because sometimes you have to talk with the kid. The caseworkers didn't know enough about group work because it was somebody else's business, as they say. So I would find that group workers who saw a kid sitting and crying under a tree would go by him, saying, "I'm not trained in interview techniques." And the caseworker would say of group work: "Well, this is a different area. It's not really therapy, it's more superficial"—which is nonsense, because it's more complex than that. So I had half group workers and half caseworkers in that class, which was delightful.

Then I developed a term—marginal interview—a miserable term, but I couldn't find a better one. It means, for example, that if I am a group worker and I have a club of 12 kids, and Mary runs out and slams the door and the rest of the kids are mad at her, somebody has to talk with her *now*. You can't wait until the caseworker comes next week. And the talk with her is much more like what you would do if you were a caseworker rather than a group worker. Just bawling her out and saying "Why don't you come back in and join the nice club" would not be enough. You have to listen and find out what is going on. So there's a lot of one-to-one interaction needed between an adult and the kids, even though you are officially the group leader.

At the same time, look at it the other way around. Mary's caseworker doesn't have to handle that problem. First of all, she won't get there until next week and, secondly, the person who brings Mary back into the group should be the one who is in charge of the group and can help Mary get rid of her anxiety or anger before she goes back into the group. You can't just say "The caseworker will handle it next week." She has other things to do with that kid. So we are really interested in where the delineation is. If I am Mary's caseworker, what will I do with the incident? Of course, if I'm around when it happens, I will do something. But if someone else is around when it happens she will also do something, and it's not a conflict between casework and group work techniques. We called it marginal interview because it's like the casework interview but it is done by the person who is in charge of the group situation.

Then I went to Washington in 1953, where I was in charge of the children's psychiatric unit in a government research hospital in Bethesda, Maryland. We had a special project where we worked with youngsters on a closed ward in a huge hospital for adults. There, obviously the word marginal didn't mean anything because we had psychiatrists, psychologists, caseworkers, group workers, nurses, and attendants. So I had to find a term that was better, and I picked up the term life-space interview because this was where the kids lived. It meant that someone who is engaged in your living process has to do the talking, or whoever does the talking has to be close to the event.

Now, at that time, Kurt Lewin used the term life space but in quite a different way. I knew him very well, we were

good buddies, but he didn't like psychoanalysis very much
and didn't like the term unconscious. What I would call
"unconscious processes in the group," he called the "hid-
den agenda." So I said, "What the hell! Why fight about
terms?" and he laughed.

*You ran groups yourself; you didn't just administer or build
theory. You were very much involved in working directly with children. There are probably many people out there who were in a group
that Fritz Redl ran. Did you call yourself a leader, a therapist, a
group worker, or what?*

I didn't have any professional name.

You were Fritz?

If I go to one of the federal prisons, there's always
somebody who says "Hi, Fritz, how are you?" My best
successes have made it to federal prisons, not just ordinary
ones!

You see, it's a complicated role. It began in Vienna,
when I was a strict school teacher as far as subject matter
went. I wouldn't just let my students pass; yet I allowed
them to call me by my first name. So even though I was a
strict teacher, the same kids would come in the afternoon
and want to tell me about their girl friends or whatever, and
it was fine. I always felt that lines shouldn't be drawn so fast
—or they should be drawn in terms of what was appropriate
at the particular moment rather than in the abstract.

Did you run your project by yourself?

I had an administrator of the camp so I didn't have to
do it all, but I was the camp director. I was the top kick as
far as the kids went. The winter groups I didn't run; Selma
and some of the other people had those groups. But sometimes I would take over if one of the group workers was
sick.

I didn't live at Pioneer House, but I was there day and
night most of the time, and Dave Wineman was sort of my
second in command. It was from the work of this project
that the books *Children Who Hate* and *Controls From Within*
emerged.

You found a home in social work? You were in education and psychoanalysis. . . . How many years did you spend at the Wayne State School of Social Work?

Eleven, I think. Let me see, it was from '41 to '53— twelve.

Your major work came out of that period. Is that because social work was receptive to psychoanalytic thinking?

That was very interesting. I think the chance mixture of my biography had something to do with it because I was accepted, and I found the social workers, especially the psychiatric caseworkers, closest to being psychoanalysts, except they don't get paid for it. So I was very much at home, and they considered me one of them. If I taught a class in casework/group work, the caseworkers were comfortable because they knew what I was talking about. The group workers were less comfortable in the beginning, and I had to do a lot of translation of language so that they would be comfortable.

Were you happy there?

I was very happy there. Professionally they were the happiest years of my life.

A very creative time. . . .

And very sympathetic. At that time, Wayne was still a city university; now it is a state university. Of course, I had a lot of difficulties in getting what I needed, but my home base—that gang at the school of social work—supported me.

Now, the whole field seems to have changed. First of all, group work practically went out of business in many places. Community organization has taken over, and this is a somewhat different angle which is important and I have nothing against it.

I can't find a caseworker anymore for a children's residential unit because all of a sudden everybody is into operant conditioning.

What do you think of it?

I see it as not only stereotyping but over-simplification and a return to simple gadgets with no concern about secondary effects, subsurface effects, long-range effects, or side effects on the group. We don't even act that simplistically with medication any more. We say, "If that thing in the bottle doesn't work, please ask your physician because maybe in your case its different."

Why is psychoanalysis losing ground?

There are many reasons why. Partly because the emotional disturbances we produce today are more complex and different than the ones we had when we originally invented our therapies. Partly for financial reasons—insurance companies don't pay for very many months of therapy, so you have to get well in a hurry. And partly because, by tradition, from a classical point of view, we are not supposed to be too interested in anything but the person's personality problem.

With children it was different from the beginning. Anna Freud would certainly give the parents advice. For instance, she would say, "You can't do this or that for punishment." Aichorn would sometimes transfer kids to the school where I was teaching, because if the kid had a sadistic mathematics teacher, how could he gain from therapy if he was exposed to a sadist? So everybody was aware of the complexity of things.

In short, in our work with children we were concerned about their other life experiences and how they were handled by adults. Only we never wrote up this area of our concern in our articles and books; we sort of took it for granted.

But the behavior therapists would tell people what to do.

Yes, they would tell them what to do. I would tell them what to do too. I would have to give parents some suggestions about what they should do. But you have to be specific in such situations up to a point, but not oversimplify. Many of these behavior management people confuse being specific with being oversimplistic.

And then there is another thing which makes behavior management popular: it becomes measurable. As social workers we always had trouble—I remember from my years at Wayne—whatever we did was never quite respected because it was not as scientific as something from the physical sciences. At that point, very few of the social workers had a doctorate, but later on more and more began to have them. That means they had to sell out to the machinery of scientific respectability, and scientific respectability in a university depends on measurability and proof. It certainly becomes proof when you can measure how many pieces of candy or how many percentages in a week—that makes it scientific! Also, they can have two groups, and they can write their thesis on comparing them, and you could never do that before. But that's another point. This is a price we paid for becoming respectable in the university community. So what makes behavior modification so popular is not so much its value in itself as the fact that it makes it possible to measure what you do.

What do you think of using drugs to control symptoms in children?

Well, many things that are done to kids are done, not just out of punitiveness but out of helplessness. In a nutshell, there is no question about the importance of the judicious use of drugs as part of a carefully thought-out therapeutic regime, as part of many other moves needed to help youngsters. What bothers me is that much of the time I find no such real planning or concern.

I am against the use of drugs as chemical warfare against unruly kids. In fact, the really serious drug research people are on my side. One does not easily know how a drug works on a kid, what else it does—or excludes from happening—after it has been administered, and we are often very unrealistic about the nonphysical realities which are important in the lives of children.

When you came from Vienna as a psychoanalyst, there were a group of you who came to the United States—yourself, Blos, Erikson. It interests me that you were all working with children. Did you work with children because you were not physicians and the psychoanalytic society here wouldn't let you work with adults? For example, Theodore Reik had a terrible time, but he was not working with children.

We personally didn't have any trouble. Neither Erikson nor Blos had trouble with private practice. And if I wanted to go into private practice, nobody would have minded because we were exceptions you know, we were from "over there," where training in child analysis began. Yet you may have a point, for the people we mostly worked with were "just kids."

With adolescents there are special problems. There aren't many who want to work with them because you cannot keep them restricted to the 50-minute hour once or twice or six times a week. You have to be around when they blow. You have to be familiar with what else is happening in their lives. You have to know their peer groups and all that. Nobody wants to touch them anyway because very few adolescents are polite enough to develop a nice obsessive-compulsive neurosis or hysteria.

Freud himself was afraid that medicine would stifle the developmental potential of psychoanalysis. Do you think that's happened?

Yes, up to a point. But group therapy has developed into quite a mature field by now.

But the psychoanalytic societies are not interested in group analysis, so they don't care.

No, but there are psychoanalytic and other schools which do endorse group therapy. Even though some of the things being done with groups are phoney, this also happened with psychoanalysis. In the early days, lots of people did many things under the label of psychoanalysis. But group therapy has grown into a mature field. There are many people who have made very scientifically and clinically sound contributions to the field. If some analysts cannot see that, that's their problem.

But I still haven't answered the question you asked. The fact that we worked with children made it easier for us, obviously; but it's not just true of the psychoanalysts, it's true for psychiatry in general. For instance, in general psychiatry the amount of attention paid to children in institutions is still very low. We don't even have a closed ward for adolescents in the one state hospital in Massachusetts! I'm trying to help them set up one, but they won't be able to do it because they're cutting expenses. They put adolescents in with adults. They have a good school program there which is privately funded, but then at 6 o'clock the children go to an adult ward and sit there for hours with nothing to do. And they're surprised that the kids get depressed again!

By the way, the premature departure of group work as a respectable unit is terribly missed because now we do not get the people who know enough about programming activities. It is just as important to know what to do with a bunch of kids in a day's time and how to handle a trip with them. All the stuff that they used to deal with, admittedly a little bit superficially, in the settlement, the YMCA, YWCA—at least they were very experienced. They weren't sensitive enough with sick kids, but they sure could recognize when kids got bored and when kids got out of hand and what materials you needed to have a good club going. Even when you use the fancy words "group therapy," you still have to have a program, whatever you mean by program. And that is now falling off too because those people are now doing behavior management and are mainly interested in giving points. They're not enough interested in the actual program, and they don't get any training in programming.

You're very interested in child-care workers.

Yes. Child care is a growing profession. It's in the state that social work was in a hundred years ago, and you guys better take it seriously as a profession, like nursing. It's a mixture of social work and nursing and group work. It's the only profession around where group work is still going on. But these people are not trained, and there's nobody to train them in most places—except some of the social work people are doing it, like Henry Meier in Seattle and Eve Citrin, who was at my half-way house, first at Pioneer House and then in Bethesda. She's training a lot of people on the West Coast.

What has happened, in your opinion, to social work?

Part of it was integrated into social action and part of it stayed, I guess, in casework. But some of it—group work —is going into behavior management, heavily (If it's still called group work, I don't know). And, of course, it's installed solidly in welfare. By the way, I think clinical psychology is now taking over what the psychiatric caseworker was doing. Clinical psychologists are getting more interested in that program, but you have to be practically 90 years old and have three degrees to be admitted because they have too few training openings.

But now everybody has discovered community psychiatry, which was what social workers did way back in 1910.

Now they're screaming for places like settlements, but they can't admit they're settlements so they have to call them community programs. I think we got poisoned by the car industry. A car has to be a new model or else it's no good, and now we do this in other areas. Any new program has to be the latest, and it's the latest only if it has a different name and is labeled innovative. The reason some of the settlement programs did not solve some problems wasn't the fault of the programs; they were never supported enough to begin with. We didn't have enough of what we needed. Now, suddenly they want something else, and they will discover after a while that much of what was done in Hull House is just as much needed now.

My last question is: Would you like to speculate on what you see as the future for group work, group therapy, social work, the behavioral sciences?

Well, if you ask me about the future, I will have to separate two issues. First of all, what do I think potential trends are? And the other question is: Will any of these trends be supported?

Right now, I think what should have happened in the field of social work may be a combination of education and the development of child care workers because as a child care worker you ought to be specially trained; it is a mixture of nursing and social casework and group work. Now the awareness of this need of training, where you have to take care of kids hour by hour, has been increased. On the other hand, they are closing down institutions. They feed everybody back to the community without asking if they need anything else. I would like to see child care work as part of a school of social work and nursing combined because the nurses need to know what the group worker knows. I think this is developing, but whether it'll be allowed to breathe or not—that's another story. Because at the same time we discover the need, our general political powers are not interested in it, and this is crazy—just like other services which we need. Everybody looks for foster homes now because institutions are out. But we know foster homes cannot work with children who are very disturbed, because what foster parent can take it? And they shouldn't. We need something else besides foster homes or we need supportive agencies like social agencies who have nothing else to do but be with those foster parents. But somehow, again we cut that out, although we know we need it. So this would be the trend, I think.

Theoretically, the trend would be in developing new conglomerations of professional skills under different titles. And maybe what previously were separate schools may have to be combined into a larger complex like child care and social nursing, or whatever it may be. And if there are enough places which are serious about taking care of kids, either in half-way houses or residential centers, then obviously the field of child care work will have to grow. The content of this field will be a blend of casework, group work, and activity programs as well as clinical skills.

The skills you need to run a program were not in social work originally. We had to steal them from the recreation guys—from the people who know what to do with arts and crafts. We had to swipe from lots of other professions and build on them. In the same way, we need a blending of skills in child-care work; the old departmentalization needs to be rearranged.

No more trinity?

That's right. It's more than a trinity by now. The field-work possibilities also have to be changed because you can't learn what you need to know in one place or the other; you need combined experiences.

Life changes. The pathologies which we produce are changing. Even in Vienna, the delinquents are already different. I was there recently, and the minister of justice of the State of Austria wanted my wife to look over the whole reformatory for the girls and me to look over the boys, which we did. We got to see lots of kids in institutions, and we were allowed to talk with them without anybody else present. It was very nice. But they don't produce the same mixture we had before; delinquents with a big need for friendly adults are no more. And the rawness of behavior has changed way beyond anything we were used to. By rawness I mean the lack of target-effect concern: if you're mad now, you smash somebody against the wall. You don't care what happens to him or to you. No more consequences, just right now. Here and now has changed everything.

Life has changed and so should the professions. We certainly can't afford the subdivisions of interdepartmental hostility that we sometimes indulge in.

But the basic ingredient in social work depends on the combining and the creating of good fieldwork placements, and that needs to be returned to again.

I suppose it's very fortunate that social work, from the beginning, had it's own schools, it's own placements, and it's own agencies. But of course there are trends in making qualifications less rigid.

I wouldn't make them less rigid. In fact, there are some areas where we know they have to become more rigid. Right now, there seems to be nothing that anybody can't do.

Maybe we need different kinds of staff, but they all have to be professional in their work, whether they are volunteers or paraprofessionals. In social work we had a beautiful concept of the professional self, remember that? It means that, just like a nurse, you can't get mad at somebody because he wets the bed again. That's why you're here, or you shouldn't be a nurse. The professional identity was strongly emphasized, it is still needed and will be needed even more.

REFERENCES

Redl, F. and Wineman D. *Controls from within: Techniques for the treatment of the aggressive child.* New York: Free Press, 1952.

Redl, F. and Wineman D. *Children who hate.* New York: Free Press, 1951.

Redl, F. Group emotion and leadership. *Psychiatry,* 1942, 5:4.

HELEN HARRIS PERLMAN is Samuel Deutsch Distinguished Service Professor, Emerita, at the University of Chicago School of Social Service Administration. Two of her best known books are *Social Casework: A Problem Solving Process* (1957) and *Persona: Social Role and Personality* (1968).

Chapter 5

HELEN H. PERLMAN

Professor Perlman, coming to Chicago to interview you, I took time to reread your paper, "Confessions, Concerns and Commitment of an Ex-Clinical Social Worker." I know you originally delivered it to the California Society for Clinical Social Work, and I understand you got a lot of commentary on it.

Yes, I did. Most of it has been very positive commentary. But of course that doesn't mean anything because the people who take pen in hand or who come up to say something to you are the ones who are largely positive. People who feel negative about your ideas tend to go off to grumble and mumble among themselves. So I don't think that any speaker or writer knows what effect he has had. It would be fun if you could fool yourself and just live off the praise.

I would assume you'd get a basically warm response.

It was a very warm response, actually. But it was an after-dinner speech, and I'm aware that after people have had a couple of cocktails and a full dinner, they're not ready to give their minds to a carefully worked out argument. So I touched on a few high spots only. But once a thing goes into print, it seems to have a kind of permanence and fixity that does not occur when one is presenting something orally. The few negative criticisms I've had have been, for example, that I didn't deal enough with the psychotherapeutic aspects of casework treatment. My defense is that the listeners were all caseworkers experienced in psychotherapy. I didn't have to tell *them* about psychotherapy. One thing I could tell them about was some of the conflict that I, who had once done counseling and treatment, still had and about that aspect of social work which I feel has been given short shrift—to remind them of the social part of social work and to share with them the concerns I had about this.

Did the criticism have to do with that very point—your key point about the "social" in social work?

Yes, that I did not speak sufficiently of the psychological or psychodynamic aspects. I certainly didn't think that with this group it would be necessary. If, for example, it had been a society of *anti*-clinical social workers, I might have taken a very different tack. One's emphasis should shift with the group one addresses, I'd say. But largely, I've had a great number of letters, in effect saying "Thank you for expressing what I've long thought." Some come from teachers of casework or of "social treatment" in schools of social work. Some have come from people in clinics, where this business of affecting the client's environment has become a major necessity for social workers and needs to be taught and thought out better.

It's true that all of us who have taught and written about the methods in social work have talked about the necessity for dealing with the client's environment. This is old stuff. And as a matter of fact, there are great numbers of published articles that tell in a condensed way that "I talked to the landlord and got him to agree that he will withold the eviction" or "I visited the school and talked to the principal and teachers, and they agreed they will try to give him more individual attention." But what I'm after is *how* was that discussed? *How* was the landlord motivated to withhold eviction? *What* happened between the caseworker and the principal and teachers? I think we have to examine this process in somewhat the same way we examined process in the one-to-one dialogue between client and worker, and we need to extract what principles govern influencing the client's peopled environment.

I found it an interesting paper, and I'm not surprised that it stirred up controversy. I think the field at this point is fermenting on just such issues as these.

I can understand the malaise that caseworkers feel as a result of the terrible beating we've taken over the last ten years and the low value put on what caseworkers have done. The earth beneath our feet began to feel very shaky, so I haven't felt annoyed at anybody who wrote me a critical letter.

What I'm after, you see, is getting at action for social change that can be carried out by the direct-service worker along with direct influence upon the client himself. Then maybe we'd come clearer about *case* action being different from *cause* action—*both* are forms of social action—and maybe we'd move from hot rhetoric to *doing*.

You're not at all "emerita," I can see.

I've been awfully lucky. I chose to retire. What I really chose was to have the freedom to work as much or as little as I wanted to, and the University of Chicago's rulings make this possible. So I'm semi-retired or quasi-retired—and thoroughly enjoying the best of two worlds, work and leisure.

Did you know that I just returned from teaching winter quarter in Hong Kong? I taught at Hong Kong University's graduate social work department and at the Chinese University's undergraduate department. This is apropos of being "emerita." Those assignments called for every ego function I had operating—every coping strategy I had because the impact of another culture and the adaptations one must make to it demand some pretty fast and fine mental footwork! I came away with tremendous new respect and admiration for foreign students who come to America for their training.

Actually, social work in Hong Kong, under British influence, is quite sophisticated. They have a good roster of agencies, and the training program in their social welfare department is highly commendable. Nevertheless, it seemed to me that there was too great adherence to western thought and western psychology, which were not always useful there. The population is 98 percent Chinese, and I felt that Chinese values and traditions had not been sufficiently taken into account. Of course, the elite in social work has been acculturated to western thought because they've been trained in Canada, Britain, and the U.S. They have gone back and said, "Look, this is 'the word'; this is the way social casework/groupwork ought to be." I began to hear from students and workers what their cases were like—what parent-child and husband-wife and family-clan relationships were like—and then I began to read very closely in Chinese philosophy and religion, which are really one and the same. There is no formalized Chinese psychology; philosophy is their psychology. I did a lot of reading also in Chinese literature. Modern short stories that came out chiefly in the twenties and thirties in the period of "realism" in fiction. As in the West, the literary works of quality reveal far more of the human condition, of how people live and act and feel, than is revealed in formulations by theorists or formal researchers. And I found I rapidly began to "think Chinese." I found there was a lot of western social work theory that did not apply, that had to be considerably modified if it was to be useful.

Can you give me an example?

Well, for example, shame is a far greater motivating feeling than guilt. What is socially *seen* and what is socially *known* about your behavior is of major importance. Social expectations, social conduct, role relationships are powerful shapers of behavior and internal feeling, more in Chinese society than in ours.

There is, for example, no concept of a God such as we have in the Judeo-Christian tradition—a God who can see into you and knows the terrible things that you're feeling or thinking. Nobody knows what you don't show, what you don't speak of. What you don't act out is unknown; therefore, you don't have to harbor guilt about it. If you hate your brother but you act nicely to him, everybody thinks you are a wonderful sister, and you think so too.

The social rules governing behavior are very clear still in Chinese society. Of course there's a tremendous change and breakup of tradition, and westernization is developing very rapidly—with some of its worst aspects emerging there.

But today, even among quite westernized young students in tight jeans and shoes with three-inch platforms, there remain strong and deep allegiances to traditions of family. Scratch the surface and you will find them. For instance, several students asked me: "Why do American children hate their parents?" When I asked, "Why do you think they do? What's your evidence?" they said they had gone to college in the U.S., and they found that American students wanted to get away from their parents just as quickly as they could. I said, "Wouldn't you, if you could? Wouldn't you like to have an apartment of your own, entertain your own friends?" "No, we like our parents; we enjoy being with them. Besides, they need us very much, because when they get old, parents are very lonely." "Are your parents old?" "Oh yes, they are very old." "How old are they?" Well, I won't tell you how old they were because they were all younger than I!

Your trip must have been exciting.

It was tremendously exciting, really mind opening. I was walking many tight ropes trying to adapt to a different culture, for all that externally it looked much the same. I was continually asking myself: "Why am I so tired?" And I realized that I not only was taking in a great deal that was new but then having to rearrange it and take some different stance in my teaching from what I was long accustomed to. Yes, it was tremendously interesting. Isn't it lovely to have work one enjoys? There is no day that I don't appreciate this. There are a lot of circumstances over which one doesn't have control that determine whether you can do that: had it not been for my mother's coming to live with us years ago and taking on the care of my child (she was a *good* mother, probably a better mother than I could have been), I don't think I could have done full-time work in practice and then in teaching.

Then your mother lived with you during the time your son grew up?

Yes, almost until he finished high school, and she was as marvelous with him as she had been with her own children.

Is she still alive?

No. You know, it was a very sad thing, but when Jonathan was in his last year of high school and came not to need her, I saw a rapid deterioration occur in her. She had lost a very vital role. She was still a much loved member of the family, but she had no real function anymore. Of course, she was growing old; her sight and hearing were failing and she said even her taste buds were failing. She had always relished people and reading and good talk and good food. But the loss of an essential role often, I think, hastens the deterioration of a person.

One hears a lot about that in connection with men retiring; I think it happens just as often to women when their children begin to leave home. But you mentioned your son, and I do want to know about him.

He is a man now. He's in a field unrelated to mine or his father's. He took his master's degree here at the University of Chicago in business administration and has since worked with an international auditing and management firm specializing in the education of its staff and clients in the uses of computers. He says, "You see, mother, I became a teacher too," "You know how it is when the students do or feel this." So we share the plagues and pleasures of teaching.

Your speaking of your mother and son is a good transition toward getting some information on your own personal background. Do tell me about it. When I was a student here, you were not a topic of general discussion; with other faculty members there were anecdotes of background and temperament, but there were no dramatic tales circulating about you.

There are still no dramatic tales. One could look at my life and say "How ordinary." But I've found it full of surprises and small pleasures.

I'm the oldest of four: one brother and two sisters. I was born and raised in St. Paul, Minnesota, in a period of great hopefulness and progressiveness and the general assumption that the world was getting better.

And in an area of great progressiveness, Minnesota.

Exactly. And my life as a child had a very sunny, open feeling about it. I speak of this because sometimes I think I'm impossibly optimistic, you see. Oh sure, there were sibling rivalries with my brother, and my fifth grade teacher slapped my face because I wanted to do long division by my mother's method rather than by hers—and because of this trauma, I became an arithmetic imbecile. But by and large, I had lots of love from a close, affectionate, extended family. I had all my four grandparents nearby until I was in college. In turn, I poured out love and my father nicknamed me Miss Mush. But my problem is, I'm never able to stay depressed.

My father was an armchair radical. He was strongly sympathetic to many of the progressive movements of the time: single tax, unionization, the IWW [Industrial Workers of the World], the right to strike, and so on. My mother too—strong on peoples' rights and responsibilities. I can remember some of the stresses my father, who was a factory manager, had in his role when he would be pitted against the union. I remember overhearing discussions he had with my mother when he said he could hardly stand it because he thought the workers were right, yet he had to represent management. I guess I first understood role conflict then!

But it never, *ever* occurred to me that I would become a social worker because I had never heard of what that was. I was going to be a writer. I started very early writing stories and poems and had a number of them published in the children's pages. I continued writing all through college, took creative writing courses, publishing in the college literary magazine.

Because I won a number of writing prizes, I hoped to go on with graduate work in English literature and to teach at the college level. In those days, in my innocence I had the illusion that if you were a teacher, you met your classes and then could spend the rest of your time writing. I didn't know about all the preparation and continuous study involved in teaching or about all those committee meetings one needs to attend—where, if you have an idea, you're made chairman and asked to draw up the memorandum!

But I didn't go on in English, and maybe the reason why is of some interest. I was very much the darling of the English department. But I was told, first in cloaked ways which I didn't understand and finally one of my teachers told me openly—I was shocked, but it was true—that I didn't stand a chance. First, I was a woman (a girl, actually.

I was 19). The opportunities for women in academic departments were practically nil. The second handicap—or maybe it was the first—was that I was a Jew, and the opportunities for Jews in academia in the twenties were practically nonexistent. I speak of this because of the tremendous changes that have taken place in the intervening years.

But at 19, how must this have struck you, even with your optimism?

Well, I was terribly disappointed. But I must also say that I have always been a realist and, I guess, have differentiated between a hurt that's personal and one that's part of a system. Anyhow, I recognized that this was a reality I simply had to yield to. But look at the change that's taken place! It's true it takes an awfully long time; I guess one problem is that God hasn't made our lives long enough! Change takes place, but often it's hard to see it in an individual lifetime. The entry rights that women have won in academic situations are remarkable, and any university catalog today shows a large number of Jews on the faculty. Two vital changes in minority group status have taken place. It gives me hope that today's most serious minority problems will also be ameliorated, given enough effort and breathing space and time.

So, then I thought I would go into advertising because I was quite intrigued with the purple prose about perfumes, fashions—all that stuff. And I thought I would do this to earn a living while I worked on the Great American Novel, you see.

To look for an advertising job, I came to Chicago, and to earn my own living while I looked, I asked for a job at the Jewish Social Service Bureau of Chicago, which sometimes took on summer workers. They hired me.

I want to tell you I hadn't the foggiest notion of what I was going to do. I inherited a shabby wooden desk with 45 case folders piled up on it, and on top of these, holding them down firmly, was Mary Richmond's *Social Diagnosis.*

The woman who said she was my supervisor said: "These are your cases, and read that book."

That was your introduction to social work?

That was it! Well, I read the book because I was accustomed to reading books; I was afraid to look at the case folders.

I knew that I really didn't know the poor or the sick or the hurt people. So I went into the field, as we used to say, and observed again in the ways I had long developed as a reader and writer to understand and ferret out peoples' actions and behaviors and feelings and problems. I think I have always had a very swift and true empathy with people —as a matter of fact, I guess with any kind of living thing. I never like to go away from home and leave live flowers there. It always seems that I'm deserting them somehow and that they'll be lonesome.

At any rate, I listened to people who seemed eager to talk and asked them about themselves and responded with genuine feeling. People told me things about their marital situations that I never dreamed of before. They told me about the trouble they were having with their kids, about how hard it was to manage on their husband's earnings. I would ask questions to help them explain themselves because I wanted to understand more fully. Suddenly I began to be aware that people found this helpful somehow. This was a funny thing, I didn't have the foggiest notion of *how* to be helpful! It never occurred to me that with my brief life experience and dealing with people who were almost all older than I and far more experienced in life, I could be helpful. I went to them quaking, thinking "What do I say if they ask me this or that?" but I found—looking at people, listening to them explain themselves, and responding to their feelings—that I seemed to be developing very strong relationships with them. This pleased me but also frightened me because I wasn't quite sure what to do with it. I got many strong transferences and didn't know what to do about them.

If I may digress a bit, I know that sometimes, as in my first book, *Social Casework* [1957], I have been accused of being too intellectual—I don't deal enough with the emotional transactions between people. Now that the smarting has gone, I can almost understand that criticism. I guess I so take the emotional interpenetrations between helper and client for granted that it seemed to me superfluous to talk about it.

Well, the agency was very kind to me and gave me several hours a week to look for advertising jobs. At the end of the summer, when an advertising job came along, I didn't want it any more. I wanted to stay in social work, and that's what I did.

My parents struggled with that but, as always, they respected my freedom. But my mother wistfully said she *did* hope that I wouldn't have to wear one of those ugly-looking bonnets!

I stayed with that same agency, learning a great deal, for about five years. Then, in 1933 the New York School of Social Work offered four Commonwealth Fellowships. They were very eager to educate people from places other than the East, and I was awarded one of those fellowships. Again, speaking of changed views, the executive of the Jewish Social Service Bureau in Chicago, Virginia Frank, who was a remarkable woman—she had not one day of training in social work, but she was a natural—tried to persuade me not to go to school because she said she thought I was a natural. I "had it" and I didn't need training. But I knew I needed it because I felt that I wanted to use whatever helping power I had in ways much better than I then knew. Too much was happening between me and my clients that seemed like a spontaneous combustion, but I wasn't able to say *why* it was happening or know what to do about it.

Today, some would say it really doesn't matter. If you're hot, you're hot. If you've "got it . . ."

If you've got it in the gut, you don't need it in the head—?

That's right. Do they tell you that now?

Oh sure. It *does* have to be in the gut, but I'm a firm believer in gut and head being connected with each other.

It works better that way.

I think so. So this is why I found my experience at the New York School tremendously stimulating and helpful. I was introduced to explanations and theories of why what I already knew experientially worked, or didn't work, and to principles that guided my action. Everything began to fall into place in an ordered, organized way. And I learned many new things too. I learned why I'd had many failures —why things didn't work—and what some of the unfathomables in human nature were that *nobody* knew about.

So it was exhilarating for me. I was lucky enough to have some of the most outstanding teachers in social work. Gordon Hamilton was one of them, and while Gordon Hamilton and I sometimes did not agree, we stimulated one another, I think, many times. Long after I left the school, we maintained an occasional correspondence about social work problems or issues. Gordon was very disappointed in me when I moved toward incorporating some of the functional school's ideas. . . .

That's right! You were in the midst of the functional-diagnostic controversy!

We had quite a split on that. At that time it *was* a major controversy. It just tore the field apart.

I can remember when I had a paper assigned on the functional school–diagnostic school controversy. I couldn't understand what all the fuss was about. It was beyond me, so I went and read your paper "The Parable of the Workers in the Field," which has been to this day one of my favorites in connection with that issue. You bring home so clearly how the workers in both fields are tilling the same soil. And

I felt that you could probably rewrite that parable for the clinicians and the activists of today.

You've put your finger exactly on the spot! When I put together the articles for my book *Perspectives in Social Casework,* [1971] the editor of the Temple University Press said to me: "This paper is on an old issue; that fight is over." But I said: "I'd like to put it in because it bears on another fight today." I was referring, of course, to the struggle over the past few years between the direct services sector of social work and the social action–social development sector. And I thought maybe the article would offer some perspectives . . .

I found it helpful. It helped me understand that controversy—as much as I ever did understand it.

Well, unimportant as it seems now, it was one of the most violent controversies in casework. Not here in Chicago; it was chiefly the New York-Philadelphia-Boston radius that was involved. I remember going to a conference in Atlantic City—I think it was in 1938—where a group of us went into a restaurant and a very bright waiter met us at the door and asked: "What side of the room do you want to sit on, the diagnostic or the functional?"

That's marvelous.

Back to teachers. Fern Lowry was a superb teacher; one of the clearest thinking people I've ever encountered. Then I had Madeline Moore, whose name is scarcely known anymore, as my field teacher. With Charlotte Towle and Fern Lowry, she was part of that first model child-guidance clinic under the Commonwealth Fund auspices. Lawson Lowry and David Levy were chief psychiatrists; they really were a clinically superior group. I am deeply grateful to those teachers.

They must have thought well of you too because you were teaching at the New York School within two or three years.

Well, you see, I came as an already experienced person. Another great influence in my professional life was Dr.

Marion Kenworthy, a psychoanalyst who really has been, since her beginnings, a *social* psychiatrist. She would stop in the middle of a seminar on psychodynamics and remind us social workers that we must not forget the *social,* not forget the environmental factors. She was quite a towering figure.

Then, when I came here to the University of Chicago as a colleague of Charlotte Towle's, Charlotte was my teacher whether she knew it or not. I learned many things from her. I've written about her influence on me in my preface to *Helping: Charlotte Towle on Social Work* [1969].

You see, I grew up in a family where intellect and teachers were respected. A teacher had to *prove* himself to be stupid before I could believe that he really was. I assumed that he had much to give me, and I wanted to get from him all I could. I guess this was one of the problems I found in the period of the student revolt. The students entering the classroom were saying, in effect: "I dare you to teach me anything." I was really rocked, because it was not simply that *I* was the subject of this distrustful approach, my whole preconception about teacher-student relationships was shaken.

Do you think it was in proportion to one's reputation that one got this hostile and rejecting conduct? You know: "The bigger the name, the harder you're going to have to teach to get through to me."

You know, I never thought of that, but it's possible. I think also that perhaps less experienced, younger teachers were more willing to give up things that they held dear because they hadn't held them dear for so long. One of the things I take as given is that if I don't know more about a subject than the student knows, then I don't have any right to be the teacher or to be drawing a salary, certainly not for simply convening and chairing a course. I don't see egalitarianism in this sort of situation as useful. I know that many of my students are far brighter than I. I know that many of them have skills and knowledge far greater than mine in many areas and that they could teach me and I would be their eager student. But if they come into a course in which the teacher allegedly has expertise, I really cannot see how or why that should be denied.

I understand many teachers had a bad time. I'm glad to see that era has past. Let's see. You taught at Columbia immediately upon receiving a master's degree?

Not quite. Before the New York School became affiliated with Columbia University, we got certificates. In the 1940s, with affiliation, we certificate holders could go back for 14 extra credits and earn a master's degree. I was already a field and class instructor when I did that.

Let me take us off on a tangent for a moment, if I may, to make an historical, not a personal comment. You know the whole spate of writings that speak of the take-over by caseworkers in the 1920s of psychoanalytic theory. This is held to have been the death-knell of social reform. And each writer now, rather than going to original sources, seems to take this explanation and perpetuates what I'm about to call a myth. Incidently, Leslie Alexander [1972] had an excellent article in the *Social Service Review* several years ago that debunked this myth, but I'd like to add my personal and clear memory about it.

When I went to the New York School the first time, 1933–34, psychoanalytic theory was practically unknown in social casework *except* in the New York-Philadelphia-Boston circuit. But there were great numbers of social workers elsewhere too, and their psychodynamic knowledge, I can tell you, was minimal. In the class in personality development given by Dr. Kenworthy—a vivid and engaging lecturer—it was whispered that some students fainted at some of the ideas expressed—just as they had in my high school gym class when our teacher drew a picture of a pear and a worm making its way towards it. And I know that the disbelief and shock Flugel's *Psychoanalytic Study of the Family* [1921] created in our class was widespread. When I returned to my agency in Chicago—one of the most advanced in the country—I was made psychiatric liaison between the agency and all the psychiatric clinics we used because I was "so informed and psychiatrically sophisticated!" That was in 1934–35.

And when I took a seminar with Franz Alexander that year, he was so impressed with my knowledge—simply by contrast with others who had not yet been to the fabled East —that he discussed with me my entering analysis for purposes of spreading the gospel. Well, I don't want to make too much of this, but I'd suggest that a lot of factors other than psychiatric interest were at play when social work moved its eyes from the external to the internal environment.

Back to 1940! I returned to New York late in 1935 to be married. I then took a job with the Jewish Family Services of New York, where I carried cases at the same time that I supervised and administered the district office in the area to which a large number of German refugees were coming. It was both a heartening and deeply troubling experience. It stimulated my early interest in the conscious, cognitive aspects of coping, though I never underestimate unconscious processes. The stimulus was the numbers of people who came, traumatized not only because of what had happened to them in Germany but by the terrible dislocation they had in coming to this country with mixed feelings, having to learn a new language and new customs and a new place and take on new roles and new identities. How they rose to all this was miraculous. And the agency itself was a model of flexibility, teeming with new ideas.

In 1940 the New York School asked me if there was any chance that I would be interested in a job that carried less prestige, and I think less salary, than the one I was holding. I decided that I would because it offered two opportunities: one, to work in Harlem with a completely different population group from those I'd known and, the other, to concentrate on teaching. The teaching was going to be increased right away because I was going to have a unit of ten students.

The Harlem experience was another kind of horizon-widener for me. It was a project for the detection and prevention of delinquency, as found in four selected schools of Harlem—schools that fed the Juvenile Court with kids who had gotten into trouble. The idea was to saturate those schools with social work and psychiatric services, psychological services, vocational training services, and so on, to see whether we could stem the tide. So I had a student unit there and carried some cases and gave some part-time courses in mental hygiene of childhood, basic casework, recording, and so on—a considerable roster of courses. How I did all this I will never quite understand. I couldn't do it anymore. I don't know whether it's because I'm more tired now, or maybe I have higher standards of what one should know and do before one dares to teach. But at any rate it was a very exacting, demanding experience.

You were carrying cases and teaching field work and taking courses and *teaching courses?*

I tell this to people now and they look at me as if to say "You must have done a pretty rotten job." Maybe I did! I had ten students in my fieldwork unit. Now, one of the ways I managed was to do a lot of group supervision. Today, that is considered to be a new idea, but this was in 1940. In group supervision, I dealt with the students' common problems—such commonly encountered problems in Harlem as client resistance: "I'm afraid of you people," "I don't want you people; don't bother me," "I have other worries than whether my child is reading in school or not," and so on. So we would deal in group discussion with how to understand resistance and how to work it through, how to engage nonvoluntary clients. Individual conferences occurred around individualized problems on cases or sometimes problems the student himself was having. I speak of this now because *"Plus ça change, plus c'est la même chose,"* you know?

That reminds me of something Charlotte Towle once said to me in her last years: "Old people don't disengage themselves because they have to pull in their energies. It's because they get so tired of seeing and hearing the same (expletive deleted) things over and over again!" What a love she was!

I feel I'm in on a detective story. Did it work? Did you stem the tide?

In the Harlem project? Not really. There were lots of reasons why. But we went in as a kind of mix between a traditional child guidance clinic and school social work. I didn't plan the thing, and I surely wouldn't have been wise enough to plan it even if they'd asked me. But now, in hindsight, I'd have concentrated on more work with the schools and with a lot of factors in the parents' lives. Instead, we tended to work along middle class child guidance lines. At least one of our psychiatrists always wanted complete developmental histories on every child. Now, you can imagine what, if any, meaning this had to a Harlem mother. First of all, she couldn't remember this child's development as being different from all her other kids. Second, she couldn't see what in heaven's name this was for. Why should she remember toilet training? How could she remember toilet training if there was absolutely nothing in her background that said to her that toilet training was important. You don't remember anything that seems unimportant.

When your major fear is the danger of not having rent or a job, in a house where there are no calendars, in a house where there is a clock that is usually slow or fast, in a culture where a child just grows like Topsy (these were recent migrants from the South) and where there has been no acculturation to the ideas of life stages and so on, mothers did not watch or record their child's development. They took care of their children: they gave them food when they were hungry, they got them to bed, they clothed them for school, sent them to school—on time hopefully—but that was *it*. So I found the traditional child-guidance mode highly questionable in the Harlem community, and I was sometimes a thorn in the flesh of the clinical team, and vice versa.

When the team gathered for a diagnostic conference— we had the traditional case conference with every team member putting in his or her findings—then you'd turn to carry out treatment plans but there was no client. We had a wonderful case study but no client because the client had wanted some action, while we wanted further under-standing. This was when my conviction grew about the need to engage the person emotionally from the first— when it became intense—and about the need to give him some small sample of helpfulness from the first. I learned a lot from that experience about intake, about waiting lists, about class and cultural considerations in the helping pro-cess.

A small example: I had believed it was only decent and respectful to let people know you were coming to make a home visit. So we sent letters to mothers saying that we had heard from the teacher that their child was having trouble in school and we wanted to try to help; we would come at such a time on such a day. We'd go out and find doors locked, shades pulled, nobody there. And it suddenly oc-curred to me that every official letter that came to most of the people we were trying to see was a bad-news letter. Every typewritten letter said "Your gas is going to be turned off, your rent is overdue, and so on." We also took cognizance of the fact that in this community, it was com-monplace for a visitor to just appear. A neighbor drops in, a relative comes by; they don't make formal appointments. It was not considered a discourtesy. So we began simply to knock on every door, so to speak, to try to get a foot in it. Often we were successful; sometimes not. But I cite this to show how little we understood class and cultural differences and how those would affect what we did from the very beginning.

I gather that you do not hold the notion that because class and cultural differences exist, helping cross-culturally and across class lines is impossible. Do you believe the helping person can make the adaptation? I have had colleagues who came from less than comfortable backgrounds say: "You simply can't understand, you cannot know. Only someone who has grown up in the slums can understand."

I think it's not so. It's true that you don't *quite* know in the gut, not quite. But it is possible to come close enough to other people—to draw from them how it is, how it feels—so that you can know their feelings. If from childhood you've read a lot, if you were joyous and wept with people even in books, you can feel with many kinds of people. One question I have thought should be asked at admission to schools of social work is: Did you ever cry or anguish over a book? If so, what was it, and why did you ache? That might tell us a great deal more about the capacity for compassion and empathy than ways we now have.

But I will also say that in the course of being married and raising a child, I often looked back to when I was single, when I thought I knew what was involved in marriage and parenting, and I realized I hadn't really known.

But you were still able to help others?

Yes, I think so. You can't duplicate every life experience, but if you really want to lend yourself to receiving the other. . .

And they are willing to lend themselves to your ignorance . . .

That's right. And this is one of the things that's useful: when a student can learn to say: "Tell me exactly what you mean. Tell me how that is. You know this better than I do." It's such a lovely thing to have a person say that to you because in our too-rapid life today, people keep saying, "Yeah, I understand, I understand." But they don't. You want to be drawn out. You want to be asked to explain, to tell how it is for *you*. It's one of the therapeutic things.

Is there anything you would change in your current life if you could?

I hope I don't sound smug saying this, but no, really nothing. I'm blessed with good health and so is my husband. (Lord, in this plastic world you can't find wood to knock on!) We agreed that we wanted to retire while our knee hinges were still working so that we could climb an acropolis if we chose, and our mental hinges, so that we could take in life at its fullest. We have strong friendship bonds and happy family bonds. So life, personal life, is good. I savor every moment of it gratefully.

What courses do you now teach?

I teach several at different times. I teach in the human behavior sequence: childhood, adulthood, major ideas of personality functions and structure. Most recently, I developed a course called "Utopia and Human Welfare," which is a great deal of fun plus a lot of hard work. As you know, when students come into social work, many of them have very passionate preconceptions of what a society should be like. Or perhaps more often, they come in with ideas of what society should *not* be like; what it *should* be like they really haven't thought through. So what we do in "Utopia" is take the most perfectly planned, ideal societies and examine them in the light of a number of questions.

For example, what *new* social problems does this "perfect" society create? What does this perfect society do to the individual? What individual freedoms are you ready to give up for a managed society? What is the conception of man and his motivations that dominates Plato or More or Skinner? One assignment that the students take on is not to write a Utopia of their own, because that would be a doctoral dissertation, but to take some one social problem in present-day life in which they have an interest and to design how they would like to see that dealt with along utopian lines. We start with Plato's *Republic* and end with Skinner's *Walden Two*.

One thing we have to examine all the time is the social surroundings. What is the time and place of this utopia? What is the *zeitgeist* that affects the way these thinkers and social reformers try to work out their problems? This, for many students, has been an eye-opener because they really hadn't looked at the social surroundings of their own society and its value system to see how it might affect what would and would not be possible in this society. Nor had they looked at how certain kinds of solutions breed new problems.

Our own history of social welfare legislation is a living example of that. A solution works for ten years and then creates its own problems.

Exactly. Take a splendid idea like compulsory education to the age of 18. It was a utopian idea, a beautiful idea. And yet we know now that something is very wrong with it: in the upper reaches are kids who psychologically stopped going to school years ago.

So it is a very lively course. Then I teach casework courses, from entry to doctoral levels, and try to get to my writing.

I saw the current exhibit of your writing in the S.S.A. lobby. Five books, over 70 papers, numerous stories about your travels and I know that these do not include your poetry or other creative efforts. Are you always writing something?

I'm always writing myself notes about what I want to write about. I have folders and folders—and I really thought long ago that when I retired this was what I'd do: I would sit down and I would write. So I opened my folders and I was so overwhelmed by what they held that I closed them again and put them away.

I do think that the really creative person—that is, a person who is going to be significantly productive—has got to be more one-tracked than I've tended to be. Maybe concentration is one mark of creativity? I've had so many interests on which I have spilled out my time and energy. But I'm not sorry. You asked if I'm always writing. Yes, I'm always writing, it seems to me, about one thing or another, in small ways.

Of all your writing—I know this is really not a fair question —of which book or article are you the most proud?

Of my nonprofessional publications, I guess I was most pleased about having a story published in *The New Yorker*. But of my professional work—*Persona*, I think. *Persona* holds in it more than I myself saw. I don't think I sufficiently developed its potentials. So when occasionally I take a look at a page or two in it, I find myself surprised or even stimulated, as if it weren't my own. I really didn't mine it for what it holds. I have a tendency, as you probably know, to collapse many ideas into a small space, and I try to write simply, which I hope does not mean simplemindedly.

Largely because of that simplicity of style, I used your Casework: A Problem-Solving Process *for my undergraduates this year.*

How did they like it?

I think quite well. Is there any way of knowing if it is still the best-selling introductory text?

It is amazing, to me. It has sold well over 100,000 copies in English alone. And it's translated into seven or eight languages and used in schools all over the world. There's been some pressure on me to revise it, but until I find that it's not proving useful, I don't want to do that. I don't think it's right to put forward a revision which only tidies up a few ideas or maybe adds a chapter or two and suggests that the old book should be thrown away and a new one bought. I'd rather do a new and different kind of book.

I think I want to do a book on coping; that would be the title, *Coping*. It would be a kind of primer on ego functioning, with special attention to the ego's conscious coping strategies and their implications for helping people to exercise those faculties. These last few years have produced a lot of research, small bits but important, on this subject.

That's one of the folders?

That's one of the folders, I'm afraid. When I agreed, for instance, as I did just this morning, to teach next fall, I thought to myself, "You are just trying to avoid writing." One has to have blocks of time. It is a terrible discipline, writing. You're alone, closed off, constantly confronted by evidence that you've not quite thought through some ideas. That's the major challenge in writing: communicating clearly with your reader. You're driven, because you want to tell what you think is useful, and you're pulled back because of doubts or interests beckoning elsewhere. It's a miserable pleasure—or a satisfying misery.

I do want to ask you about what you see, from your own vantagepoint, as the most important part of your work in the field of social work, if you could pick out one.

I'm not sure I can. I can tell you what I tried for, but whether I was even able to achieve what I tried for remains for others to decide. So I'm going to try to answer you honestly but with some discomfort. I think in my work I have been concerned chiefly with the everyday lives of everyday people, trying to understand them better in order to help them better.

I've been absolutely dogmatic about not being dogmatic! I've continuously tried to learn and examine what is real and true and valid and relevant for particular people in particular situations. This is what I had to do when working in Harlem. This is what I had to do when I began to be exposed to some of the thinking in the functional school years ago. My effort has been always to take from existing theory those ideas that rang true for me on the counter of practice and life experience—things that seemed to me to be most usable, most workable. I think utilitarianism is a very important and necessary value in a profession and that, elegant or intriguing though an idea may be, we've got to ask: "Is it useful, applicable, efficient, in *this* situation for *this* person?"

Today, of course, a good deal of theory from the so-called Freudian and Rankian orthodoxics has merged. This is because ego psychology comes closer to the Rankian "will" concept than did the earlier id psychology. And because Rank, whether he knew it or not, was an existentialist. And because the best of the functionalists, at least those who influenced me, had come up through Freudian training and could not, try as they might, disown all they knew. And because there *are* many commonalities among theories of human behavior. But those of us who said that years ago were severely punished for it!

I'm off the subject, but it does relate to my book *Social Casework: A Problem-Solving Process,* which presented an eclectic position on casework. I guess I'd list that as a contribution.

Professor Perlman, you've clearly sought always to be an integrator. Do you think a good social worker can hew only to one school of thought?

Let me go at that round about, will you? As I said before, I'm dogmatically averse to dogma. To me it bespeaks rigidity and constriction, and you wonder what insecurities or maybe inertias lie beneath it. There's so much we don't know about human beings and the forces they transact with. "The world is so full of a number of things," you know? At the same time, I believe in the necessity to know in depth at least one coherent and systematic explanatory theory. You've got to have some solid-core knowledge. Then, if you want to depart from it or add to it or subtract, you know your core, your starting place. I'm honestly troubled by the fragmentation and faddishness that's going on in the clinical sector of social work today— the taking on of methods that sound easy or tricky and the lack of clarity about why.

One more question: What do you see as the future of the social work profession?

I was afraid you'd ask that! My crystal ball is as clouded as the next man's, whether by anxiety or myopia, I don't know. I know I don't dare predict long range. So I'll venture tentatively, timidly, on short-term future. OK?

It seems to me there are two conflicting trends which may leave us in a kind of a stalemate. The worldwide economic crisis today, the whole pull-in-our-belt trend, which has its objective as well as subjective impacts, may cripple the social services for a time. Social work expanded and flexed its muscles in our economy of abundance. Now are we entering a scarcity economy? And yet, at the same time, paradoxically there seems to be a rising need or wish in the population at large for finding some greater personal happiness or self-realization. I am continuously astonished at the numbers of people seeking some form of releasing or therapeutic help. So I think clinical social workers will be kept busy for some time to come. Will an economic depression lessen personal psychological concerns or illusions, I wonder? I know war does.

Then also, in an increasingly complicated, bureaucratic, impersonal society there is an increasing need for interveners—people who are trained to help you navigate the channels to medical care and economic provisions and home care and insurance rights and so on. So I think direct-service personnel, many of them paraprofessionals or aides given supervision by qualified social workers, will be continuingly necessary to people in trouble.

And the need to change and improve many agency programs and policies and to create new kinds of services too will be met, I hope, not only by "cause actions" in the large, general sense but also by "case actions" in relation to individual cases that are instances of more general needs. We must pay a lot more attention to that.

You know, sometimes I'm glad I'm as old as I am. But sometimes I hope I'll be around a while before I shuffle off these mortal coils. I'd like to see how things come out!

REFERENCES

Alexander, L. Social work's Freudian deluge: Myth or reality? *Social Service Review,* 1972; *46,* 517–538

Flugel, J. C. *Psychoanalytic Study of the Family.* London: International Psycho-analytical Press, 1921

Perlman, H. H. Confessions, concerns and commitment of an ex-clinical social worker. *Clinical Social Work Journal,* 1974, *2,* 221–229.

Perlman, H. H. *Persona: Social role and personality.* Chicago: University of Chicago Press, 1968.

Perlman, H. H. *Perspectives in Casework.* Philadelphia: Temple University Press, 1971

Perlman, H. H. *Social casework: A problem-solving process.* Chicago: University of Chicago Press, 1957

FLORENCE HOLLIS is Professor Emerita of the Columbia University School of Social Work in New York. Her best known book is *Casework: A Psychosocial Therapy.*

Chapter 6

FLORENCE HOLLIS

There was an anniversary recently, the twenty-fifth anniversary of the doctoral program at the Columbia University School of Social Work. I understand you had been part of that program since its inception.

Not quite. They started planning it, apparently in '45, and I went to the school in '47. But it didn't get into action until 1950. The formative years were '45 to '50. When I got to the school in '47, I was a newcomer so I had very little to do with it in those early years. Eve Burns was the person who really designed it, and Gordon Hamilton was certainly on the committee and had an important part in it—also Phil Klein and Clara Kaiser. But Eve Burns, I think, had the major responsibility for designing it.

The students came in 1950. It took them five years to get the program through the university and get funding for it and all that. I was there after it got planned.

But eventually you became a part of it?

I think it was around '52 or '53, because I remember going over Gordon Hamilton's notes about then and she must have taught in the program for a couple of years. Lucille Austin, I think, was teaching casework in it from the beginning, if I remember correctly, so it must have been '52 or '53 when I got into it.

What was the philosophy around the doctorate, and would you comment on how you think it has evolved in a quarter of a century?

It always had a pretty strong social science–social planning emphasis, as would be natural with Eve's having planned it. It also always had a clinical emphasis. There had been two major streams. I'm trying to think carefully about what I'm saying because, in a measure, it achieved what I wanted it to achieve, and in another sense we haven't achieved what I had hoped. What we have achieved has been that we always kept the clinical in; I think we have more clinical than most of the other schools except for Smith and Pennsylvania. Those two have had the most; Chicago has also had some. I haven't been close enough to Chicago to know what their balance is.

We've kept it in, but it's never been as strong a clinical course as I would have liked it to be. It's always been a series of compromises because the social policy emphasis was so strong. And also there has been a need to have a program that would be understood and respected by the academic departments in Columbia. So we put very heavy emphasis on having a large amount of social science and a large amount of research. Much of the student's time has gone into that.

Then there's been so much new material and new theory coming into the field that we had to take a lot of time covering that and trying to evaluate these new trends, new theoretical background, and so forth, which was proper. What I'm trying to say is that we needed more time for the clinical because my experience has been—and I think other people will back this up—that recently, even the students coming into the doctoral program with a clinical interest are only occasionally, let's say about a third, really highly skilled practitioners.

What about the other two-thirds?

The other two-thirds in recent years have only had a couple of years of practice before entering the doctoral program. We've had a three-year minimum, but a number of exceptions to this have been made. Some have come from schools where they haven't had an awfully solid clinical foundation in their master's work, and then they haven't necessarily been in good agencies after they got out. I don't mean to say that they're poor practitioners, because we wouldn't take them if we thought they were poor practitioners, but neither are they highly skilled practitioners. Others have been in teaching for quite some time and are removed from practice. Again, they knew it once but they haven't practiced the new ideas. They're good people. I'm not trying to say they're inferior people; I don't mean that. But many are not necessarily highly skilled practitioners.

I had hoped that while the doctoral program would not have as its *only* aim the production of skilled practitioners, it would be a way in which some students could develop a great deal of casework skill. My own belief is that there is an enormous gap between what we really *know* in casework and what most practitioners are able to *use*. In fact, I think one reason many of the research studies come out negatively is exactly this: the general level of work is far removed from what the very best people can do and are doing.

When the program was instituted, did it have these two divisions: a clinical part and an academic research part?

It had three streams originally: it had the old community organization, later social planning, group work, and casework. There were also a few who majored in research itself. There were never many group workers who wanted to concentrate on group work. Remember this was back in the fifties. The group worker tended to take the social planning CO type of program. So you had really two streams, with very few people in the group work or research sequences. But the research and social science courses required of everyone fitted better into the CO/social planning stream than they did into the casework stream. Therefore, there wasn't enough time available in the program to move students as far along in the practice direction as I would have liked to see them move.

You then were identified with the practice part of it?

Yes, but I believe it is very important for us to have good and suitable research in practice. To do that, the research must be more closely tied in with clinical problems.

From what you have said, the beginning of this program was an attempt to produce an elitist or highly qualified person: in other words, the person who came out of this doctoral program 20 years ago, I presume, was looked upon as someone who would move into some leadership or very contributory professional role.

Definitely so. I think it is a good program, but it attempts to cover an awful lot, with the result that there has not been an opportunity for students to get as intensive growth in the clinical aspect as I would like to have seen.

I would have preferred to see more very skillful practitioners come out of the program. But I also hoped—and to a certain extent it has happened—that we would develop teachers and researchers and writers who knew practice thoroughly and could really give clinical leadership because they were on top of the best that was being done in the field.

I think that, at the beginning, our expectations of what you could do in a doctoral program were too high. That's a mistake we made, as a matter of fact, when we thought that these extra years of study would produce leaders. We don't produce leaders. Certain people whom you hope have leadership potential come in and get more information and some more skills in writing or teaching. They may or may not turn out to be leaders.

Do you think there is now a trend to the other extreme—to make expectations too low in a doctoral program?

I don't think this is true in the programs I know. I am very much concerned, however, about the move that is occurring in the direction of turning the master's into a doctorate just by changing the name. The present tendency to put much of the content back into the undergraduate years and then not to build on this at the graduate level but rather to put a one-year masters on top, I very much disapprove of. I am also exceedingly distrustful at this point of substituting a doctor's degree for a master's degree when you're not going to upgrade the master's content very much.

Speaking as a practitioner, would you want to speculate why we are doing the exact opposite of what every other profession does —namely that when you establish yourself as a profession, you upgrade your requirements.

Like everything else, it has a lot of causes. However, I want to say that we make a mistake in saying it's *the* trend. It certainly is a very strong trend at the moment, but there are countertrends going the other way. And sometimes you can get yourself into self-fulfilling prophecies by taking the thing that is talked about at the moment and assuming there are no counterforces that are going to reverse it.

Why are we on this trend? It's partly because we expanded so fast. We had a swing forward in the thirties. We got to the two-year level around 1930. We absorbed a lot of new ideas in the clinical field throughout the thirties and forties. Then, after the War came the big expansion, with the Council of Social Work Education working hard for more and larger schools. The schools were getting grants through NIMH. It was probably in the fifties and sixties when most of this occurred. And many doctoral programs were starting at the same time. The council felt, and rightly, that we had to expand at a great rate. But with expansion you run the risk of dilution, don't you? Even with the expansion we had up until the Nixon Administration, we were by no means filling all the jobs we needed to fill.

The jobs in public assistance were mostly filled by untrained people. I think there were only seven percent trained personnel in there, and those were mostly in supervisory and top executive jobs. The best educational level you could hope for with that huge mass of public welfare workers was the B.A.

If I remember correctly, it was around 1964 that the federal public assistance group began to put much in the way of money into fellowships for workers in public assistance. Then a lot of money was poured in, and there were something like 200 people at the Columbia School alone in a couple of years who were on public welfare fellowships or supported with their salaries while they were in school. But prior to 1964, while there was money in the child welfare field for fellowships, there had been very little money for this in the public assistance field.

So we had a great mass of workers, some of whom were positive toward social work ideas and some of whom were anything but positive toward social work ideas. The reason I'm bringing this in is that I think it is one of the elements that contributed to NASW's willingness to recognize a large number of B.A. people as eligible for membership. This inevitably influenced the stance of NASW toward undergraduate education, which in turn also influenced the council to support it. The undergraduate programs were feeding people into public assistance anyway, and the general feeling was that they could do a better job if they were tied in with social work. If we brought all these people together, maybe we could exert leadership through social work ideas to influence the kind of workers who were produced by the undergraduate programs and also the attitude of public assistance workers toward people who had more training.

Personally, I didn't favor lowering the M.A. requirements for NASW membership. To me it seemed like a
lowering of standards. I had been through the fuss and the
struggle in the twenties and early thirties, when we finally
got the two-year standard through, and the last thing I
wanted to see was backtracking. I also felt very strongly at
the time of the Boehm report that I didn't want an undergraduate professional degree at all. And I didn't favor cutting seriously into the amount of general education that
people were getting in college before they started to concentrate on pre-social work subjects. I think a well-
designed pre-social work course is all right, but I would
rather have it pre-social work than the first professional
degree.

However, you asked why all this happened. After
World War II, there was a great decrease in leadership
given by women in the clinical field. The emphasis on having families was very strong. The feeling was against com-
petitiveness on the part of women and a kind of softening
down, I think, of high vocational aspirations for women.
This had a very real influence on social work. You no
longer got many women who were willing to take or even
prepare for leadership responsibilities, as had been true
before World War II. Between the two wars, there had been
something comparable to our present Women's Lib movement in that women were getting the first taste of careers.
To really put yourself into your work—give it first place—
then was considered a fine thing to do.

That was my own generation of social workers. And for
the most part the direct treatment or clinical aspect of
social work had been developed by women rather than by
men. There were exceptions, of course; but on the whole
that was true.

Then the changing of AASW to NASW and the bringing in of many C.O. and group workers who had not previously been members coincided with what amounted to a
sort of partial vacuum in casework leadership. It was very

natural for community organizers who had the ability to step in. Organizational leadership is their job and they're trained for it, and we were more or less willing to sit back and let them do it. The same thing was true of deanships. I turned down several deanships because I didn't want to be an executive. It was much more interesting to teach. And I'm sure other women did the same thing. We left a kind of vacuum, which was filled by non-clinically trained people, and now we're reaping the results.

When I was on the Council of Social Work Education board for a few years recently—just before my retirement —there were very few board members who had had any substantial amount of experience in either teaching or practicing casework. The board consisted predominately of men and a few women who were either deans or other types of executives or teachers of nonclinical subjects. There simply wasn't enough input from people who had had long clinical experience and affiliation.

This is a very interesting idea. I suppose one might say, clinically, that with the influx and rise of power of the men in social work also came a more masculine psychology, of bigness and strength.

True. But I think it was also the fact that men who came into the field were much more apt to come from the social planning and organization side of things, and therefore they saw it in those terms. Often, women who had come through that side had a great deal of leadership too, so you got an inbalance in the profession. But actually that group was numerically small. I'm sorry it happened that way. But I don't think they should be criticized for it, because they took the leadership when there weren't people with clinical background around to do it.

From what you're saying, there was no struggle.

There wasn't much of a struggle over leadership. In a way, we were glad to let them take over. Later on, when it came to the issues, there was definitely a struggle, but by then we weren't strong enough to be effective.

What are the counterforces that you spoke about before?

I think the *Clinical Social Work Journal* is one. Also the societies of clinical social workers are an important part of it.

You must be aware of this unfortunate trend of social work being the "easy" entrée to the mental health field and that people see this as a way of avoiding training and have no commitment to social work?

Of course. This is one of the reasons I prefer to keep a two-year master's program and build it on the undergraduate work. I don't want to duplicate what is taught on the undergraduate level. There are plenty of ways other than giving advanced credit, which is what many schools tend to do. They're giving advanced credit and thereby reducing the master's work to one year. I don't want anybody to have to repeat in graduate school what they've had in their undergraduate work, and now the undergraduate program is so strong that it may be here to stay, so we must find ways to build on it. What we ought to do is to waive courses that seriously overlap with what students have had but require the same number of graduate points, for which they would take more advanced work. Sometimes students do get what is equivalent to first-year graduate courses as an undergraduate. OK. Then give them the equivalent of our present second-year material in their first graduate year. In the second year, move them on to the equivalent of our third year, which is now in the doctorate, and that will make room in the doctoral program for really advanced work. What I'm hoping—let's put it this way—is that there will be countermoves to keep the two-year masters, or at least almost the two-year masters, and go on building on that.

To go back to the many factors that have influenced what's happened to us in social work education: One is that the great expansion of the schools meant a tremendous demand for new faculty. By the time that the doctoral programs were beginning to produce graduates, the doctoral degree had become a primary requisite for any kind of advancement and therefore for decent salaries in schools of social work. Our graduates in the 1960s would get any number of offers long before they had their degree. By the time they finished their exams and we expected that they would qualify and be capable of doing a dissertation, they would have six or seven good teaching opportunities, often at better salaries than our own faculty was getting. They got these offers even if they were very young people who had not had much in the way of practice experience and almost nothing in the way of supervisory experience. So such students were in semileadership or even leadership positions long before they were ready for it.

Also, I think Columbia along with Smith and Pennsylvania and Chicago were the schools that were giving the most in the practice area. There were a lot of other schools whose doctoral teaching faculty had very little in the way of clinical and sometimes even social work experience in their doctoral faculty. Again, this was partly because there weren't enough social workers who had higher degrees, and often the ones who did had taken their work either in research or C.O. or social planning. A number of other faculty members had gotten social policy or sociology doctorates or some other academic degree and then had come to teach in the schools of social work. The latter group knew social work only by association with colleagues, not from having done it.

To finish that idea: I think that a lot of the other schools gave less in the practice area than we did at Columbia. So you had a lot of graduates of other schools who had nothing or very little in the way of advanced practice or advanced practice theory. These people then moved into faculty positions instead of following the earlier pattern, which was for clinical teaching staff to move in first through student supervision so that they were seasoned supervisors

before they became teachers and had been good practitioners before they became supervisors. Now we were getting
people who had had (this was true during the sixties and
it's still true) a lot of book learning, which is valuable in
itself, but had not had this grounding of practice, supervision, and then teaching. The experienced supervisors without doctoral training could no longer come into a favorable
situation because they had little hope of tenure without
doctoral degrees and at least a few publications.

I had in mind two other points—and they are important ones. Much of the research done in the fifties and
sixties tended to be evaluative research, and a lot of it came
out pretty negative. Gordon Brown's Chemung County
study [1968], which was financed by NIMH, compared the
work of regular public assistance staff with that of two caseworkers who had never been in public assistance before nor
ever worked in the county in which the study was made.
Furthermore, this county had almost none of the social
resources that a social worker would normally rely on for
bringing improvement in dealing with practical, largely environmental problems. Hardly a good set of conditions for
demonstrating improvement!

A lot of those early studies were designed by people
who didn't know practice—and during a period when we
were terribly enamored of a narrow type of scientific meth-
odology. We had only rather recently learned the tools of
careful research and were still very naive about applying
them. So we did a kind of ritual about statistical methodol-
ogy without sufficient concern as to what we were really
measuring, whether our measuring tools were really well
adapted to the kinds of data available, whether goals were
appropriate, whether treatment was even given for the
problem measured. This is a great big subject in itself,
obviously. With a few exceptions, these findings were
highly controversial. But the result was to bring a great deal
of doubt into everybody's mind—and particularly into the

minds of the doctoral students—as to whether what they called traditional casework really had any effectiveness at all. I think this had a big influence because it undercut the confidence that people had in the casework method. And then, of course, the Nixon Administration completed the undercutting.

Let me ask you about practitioners not teaching and teachers not practicing. You have been in teaching and you've been a practitioner. How did you resolve this for yourself?

Probably with a lot of overtime. When I first started teaching, I was half-time in teaching and half-time in practice, so that was no problem. Then I got my doctorate; it was actually in social work, though technically in abnormal psychology and social economy. That's what the degree at Bryn Mawr was called at that time. But it was in the school of social work, which in 1940–41 gave freedom for a dissertation in casework practice and allowed me to take some further work in psychiatry and casework along with a lot of other things. I spent two full years at Bryn Mawr—though at that time the course work could have been finished in less time—in order to practice part-time. Then I came to New York and edited *Social Casework* for five years. That was enough to convince me that editing wasn't what I wanted. It was a very interesting experience but pretty far from direct practice. I was also finishing my dissertation. Then I got back into teaching in '47 and very, very soon felt the lack of recent practice.

I realized that practice was essential for me. I am very fortunate that I live with Rosemary Reynolds, who has been in practice all along. She was in the Community Service Society at that time, when it had an excellent direct-service program. So I had a constant feed-in through her of what was happening in the field. In about '48 or '49, she made it possible for me to return to practice. She was at that time a district secretary and was able to get permission for me to practice one night a week. But even in one night a week, you learn a great deal. I usually carried a few cases, and it also gave me access to the thinking of practitioners in the district. I could get in on case conferences and psychiatric conferences when I wanted to and so forth. I did that right up until I retired. And I really do believe that anybody who is teaching in a clinical sequence must get into practice to do a good job. Many other people will confirm this. The few people who have done it have said how much of a difference it makes in their teaching, and others would like to do it if they could just swing it.

I was talking recently to one of our graduates, who is a dean of a school of social work and who is now temporarily the acting head of his university. He was saying that he carries *a* case even now. This is all he can manage for the present, but at least it is one case. Another interesting thing he said is that he is now convinced, from his present vantagepoint, that the faculty at the school of social work carries a *much* heavier load than the other faculties. Almost any social work teacher will tell you this is true—at least for the methods teachers.

And here is another factor. The faculty that has to do with practice courses also has to take responsibility for fieldwork, and it takes an enormous amount of time to look after those students in fieldwork. We also have much more in the way of conferences with students. We're terribly overloaded. The people who are not doing any field advising are sometimes very busy too, but they are not quite as pushed and therefore they have more time to take on writing and research tasks. Yes, it's a structural thing. Mitch Ginsberg has tried awfully hard to free our time. And then came the shortage of money, and the faculty had to take on even heavier loads, and they're just dreadfully pushed at Columbia now. I'm sure that's true of other schools.

Where did you get your masters?
Smith.
And was social work your first career?

Yes, I went right into it. I had a sociology major, which is one of the reasons I don't have all that awe of sociology. Sociology has changed a great deal since those days, but I don't have the feeling that it's so superscientific in comparison to social work. I think that they're groping and trying to find out the same way we are. I don't think they have any more answers than we do. I do think they've made contributions, but they haven't made *all* the contributions.

However, just by accident, one of my instructors at Wellesley pushed me into a summer program called Junior Month that was run by Clare Tousley here in the New York COS [Charity Organization Society, later the Community Service Society] for quite some time. A certain number of college juniors were brought into the agency for a month. So I found out about social work through that experience and was quite thrilled about it. It was just the beginning of the move away from advice giving and the beginning of psychoanalytic understanding. It was in 1927 or the end of 1926 that it started here in New York. It was all brand new to me. I had had a little bit of modern psychology in college, and here it was—in action. I found it a very freeing, exciting experience.

So the next year I got an apprenticeship, and that started it. I had two years of apprenticeship in Philadelphia. This included courses at Pennsylvania under Robinson and Taft and Karl deSchweinitz. This was before Robinson and Taft were functional; they were in the in-between state at that point and had not yet been analyzed by Rank. They were very interested in Rank's ideas, but hadn't become really functional.

I was working at the Family Society in Philadelphia under Betsey Libbey. Margaret Millar, who I had as supervisor, also supervised students for Pennsylvania School, so I had very good supervision. It was a very exciting time. Then Karl deSchweinitz called me down to his office one day and said: "You should get a degree. Why don't you go

to Smith? You can get a degree in a little over a year there."
So I did, and the agency financed it, which was nice.

Then, after Smith the Depression was on us—that was
'31 and social work was expanding. The private agency was
doing the basic relief job, as we used to call it. They needed
new staff and Betsey Libbey was very much in favor of
training. There was a handful of recent graduates in the
agency. Pennsylvania School had just started its two-year
course. We were all pushed ahead like mad, and I was made
a district superintendent the year I graduated from Smith.
I stayed there until '33. Then I went out to Cleveland as
district secretary and got a chance to teach part-time at
Western Reserve. I was there seven years.

It's funny the way people influence you. Leah Feder,
who was teaching casework by then at the George Warren
Brown School at St. Louis, had been a district secretary for
many years at the COS here in New York and also had a
background in child welfare. She said to me: "If you're
going to stay in teaching, you'd better get yourself a doctorate." And she was quite right. So I did.

Who was most influential in your life?

Professionally? Well, Betsey Libbey I'd put at the top
as far as providing an atmosphere in which it was possible
to grow. She died a couple of years ago at age 80. She was
in the family service movement; she was the person who
took over Mary Richmond's seminar. Do you know how
much influence those seminars had?

That's a big, interesting story. Back in the teens and
early 1920s, Mary Richmond ran a summer institute that
went on for a month to which a small group of selected
people was invited from family agencies all over the country. It was tied in with the organization that later became
the Family Service Association of America. When she was
writing her famous book *Social Diagnosis,* she based it very
much on cases brought in by various members of these
groups. These institutes created a kind of inner core of

people who were interested in bettering social work methods and casework methods. By the way, Mary Richmond was very sound in recognizing the effects of both the environment and what she called personal characteristics. But she was too early for modern psychology. She thought Freud was terrible!

Did you know her?

I think I met her once, but she died in 1928 from cancer. Then Betsey Libbey took over the seminars. They continued a very important part of the whole family service movement.

Betsey had become interested in psychoanalysis. She carried the seminar for only a few years, and then they decided to break it up into regional seminars because it had gotten so big. She helped to bring a number of very good analysts to be among the teachers at those seminars. She never fell for any idea that the analyst would be *the* teacher of the caseworker. She was always clear that what the caseworker did was not what the analyst did but believed that an awful lot could be learned from analytic psychology. She created a good atmosphere for her staff. She gave you time to write papers—not that you weren't supposed to get your job done too. She'd also help you to find a place where you could get published. A very creative person. And she pushed young people along, perhaps faster than they should have been pushed, but it was great for young people. She was a good teacher herself, she really knew casework, was progressive and open-minded.

Margaret Rich, then editor of *The Family* (later *Social Casework*) helped me get started writing because she was willing to take a chance on a young person. When I started writing my first book in '36, I had only been out of school five years, but she encouraged me to go ahead. I sent her a chapter showing what I had in mind. It was a lousy chapter, and in the end I didn't use it, but she saw the good things in it and said: "Go ahead, keep working on it. You have an idea." I think it's terribly important that people who are farther along take some interest in younger people and encourage them—encourage them to do things and have confidence in themselves. That was very important for me.

What about personal influences?

That's too hard a question to answer. Ask my analyst.

Your undergraduate work was where?

Wellesley.

Are you from New England?

No, Philadelphia. Again, I was terribly lucky. My family didn't have much money, and no girl had gone to college before. A couple of them were teachers but they had gone to Normal School. The family wanted me to go to the University of Pennsylvania. And then a YWCA secretary, Mildred Dougherty, at a summer camp asked me where I was going. And I told her, "I guess I'll go to Pennsylvania," though I was not all that keen about it. She said, "Why don't you get yourself wherever you want to go?" And I said, "I don't have enough money." She said, "There are scholarships around. Make up your mind to try, and you can get somewhere else." Then things just opened up. A teacher in high school asked if I had ever thought of going to Wellesley. Well, it just happened that Wellesley was a place I had heard about and wanted to get to. I was just getting very average grades, so she said: "Well, see what you can do with your grades, and maybe I can get a scholarship for you." So I started to work like a dog, which I hadn't done before, and got my grades up. Graduated second in the class or something of the sort—it was because people had said something that gave me a real reason.

How did your family feel about it?

Oh, they were really lovely about it. They were very supportive. They were very sad about having me go away because it wasn't in their tradition to have a child go away to college. But both Mother and Dad were fully supportive.

Dad loved cars and he didn't have enough money to get one. You know, in those days everyone didn't have a car—this was way back in '24—and he had just gotten to the point where he had enough money and was going to get himself a car. He spent the money on me instead.

Were you from a large family?

No, but Dad didn't earn a lot of money. He was an accountant, and in those days accountants didn't bring in all that much. There was just my brother and me, but in those days it wasn't easy to go to college.

Some of our relatives thought: "What are they doing that for, when she could go to Pennsylvania?" I think Dad's family really favored it because that was the side that had the teachers in it. Mother's family thought she was nuts to let me go, but she was very much in favor of it.

To get back to social work: speaking a little simplistically, one might say there is a functional school, there is a psychosocial school, and somewhere in the middle is the problem-solving approach. You are a major articulator of the psychosocial school. Would you address yourself to that?

It actually is the tradition that came to me from Betsey Libbey and the FSAA group that worked with her. A number of people who started on her staff later became agency executives and case supervisors and practiced from this point of view in their agencies. Then there were many other leaders: Gordon Hamilton was the outstanding writer and educator here in New York; Lucille Austin taught and wrote. Another was Fern Lowry. Florence Day, first in Cleveland and later at Smith. Annette Garrett at Smith. Charlotte Towle was a major leader and was also close to the problem-solving approach. Helen Perlman was the one who tried to bridge the functional-psychosocial gap with problem solving.

At present, I think what we have are derivatives, and our views have modified to a certain extent. You see that a lot of people who were mainly identified with the psychosocial point of view are now recognizing greater value in selective use of time-limits, for instance, than would have been true even ten years ago. So there isn't the same degree of alienation between the two points of view as there was in the earlier days. I don't think, however, that the psychosocial has by any means absorbed the whole Rankian point of view. Rather it has softened its own edges and has taken over some of the techniques that the Rankians found useful when it also found them valuable. The existential group—don't ask me what I mean by that because I'm using the word as loosely as everybody else does—the group that emphasizes the here-and-now is, in a way, close to the Rankians. And I think a lot of people who started out as Rankians find that point of view congenial because one of the things they still don't like is the idea of diagnosis or assessment or of doing much about trying to get at understanding what might have caused something or contributed to it.

I don't hear much anymore about pure functionalism. Instead, I hear about some of the same ideas in short-term treatment and in some of the more or less existential type of things.

Why do you think the functional people are more comfortable with an existential approach?

Because they always did emphasize the present. The here-and-now part is existential. They also were impatient of anything in the way of history, and the existential group doesn't feel that it's important either, as far as I can see. I think those are probably the two chief things.

Do you think these casework models are outmoded, or will they simply be transformed in some way?

No, I don't think they're outmoded. I think they're going to live together for quite some time, and I think they're all going to change as time goes on. There's a certain core that they all hold in common.

You know, my research has demonstrated very well that the actual, central focus of psychosocial casework is what's going on currently. A lot of casework is not involved with behavior change at all, and quite properly so. There are problems to be solved, there are practical things to be done, and so on. But where it is involved with an effort to change behavior, even in a minor way, it's done primarily by looking at what's going on now. What's happening between the client and the people he's dealing with, between the client and you, the worker; this is the data. My research and that of others closely related to it has shown conclusively that the amount of time that actually goes into real reconsideration of early life—I'm talking about real *use* of that history, not as part of the caseworker's understanding but as part of the client's getting insight into it—is very, very small.

Now, I'm sure that there are exceptions to that. But Helen Pinkus's analysis of material which came from both family agencies and psychiatric clinics came out with very similar results, line by line, of what really went on in the interviews. And it doesn't mean that the early history isn't important. When the client's problem is one that might be affected by early life experiences, you do explore—if he is willing to talk about it. And if it will help him to function better, you do what you can to promote his insight into his feelings and actions and some of his formative experiences. But this is in addition to helping the client to look at what's happening now and see what his contribution to it was and whether he misunderstood the other person. And helping him too to understand other people—what he does to them, why they feel and act as they do, and so on.

But that requires a theoretical conceptualization. Otherwise, you don't know what to do with it.

Yes, exactly. You have to have a theory of personality dynamics and development to help you understand what is going on so that you can help the client himself to understand. The psychosocial school makes use of personality theory from a number of sources but relies most heavily on modern psychoanalytic theory, with emphasis on the way the ego and superego function. This is not pure ego psychology; it's an emphasis on ego functioning against the background of an understanding of the broad general dynamics of personality and its development. It does not accept the idea that *only* the present is important, and it does maintain that you can help more effectively if you assess what factors are contributing to the client's troubles as a guide to counteracting their force.

Your own sense of integrating the history of our profession with an understanding of the present has come through very clearly in our talk. I wonder if you would speculate now on the future of social work. Is history repeating itself now, and are we headed for separatism?

Separatism? I hope we're not headed for that! As a total profession, we can attack many different sides of our society's problems—that is, if we pull together. Our different approaches can modify and supplement each other and keep us all closer to reality. But we must have specialization within social work. The generalist idea is too simplistic. It may or may not be a place to begin in training, but if we don't go any further, we'll be full of jacks-of-all-trades who don't know any of our approaches thoroughly. We do need new ideas and experimentation, but these should be built on the best of what we already know. They shouldn't be just naive reruns and warmed-over methods found inadequate long ago. We very much need specialization on the doctoral level: the clinical doctorate and a comparable one for advanced work in social planning, administration, and so on.

Another thing. Women can't sit back and expect men to do all the fighting for this. There are now many good men practitioners. Some of them have worked hard on this problem and given leadership. But men aren't in the majority in this large branch of social work. Women will have to become more active and skillful in educational and organizational leadership, in teaching, writing, and research if clinical practice is to advance and to regain its rightful place as a highly skilled social work discipline.

This is worth fighting for—no other clinical group has as much commitment to counseling and providing other individual help of good quality to the poor and the near poor. No other group has gone as far in trying to understand the psychological differences that go along with poverty. Also, social work has a better hold than any other profession on the organizational means for giving these services. If the clinical group pulls out, all individual services in social work will be terribly, terribly weakened. What we need is not clinical separatism but a good stiff fight for strengthening the clinical specialization *within* social work—some specialization in an upgraded master's program and a big push forward on advanced work at the doctoral level.

If we can work that out, then I'm optimistic about the future of social work.

REFERENCES

Brown, G. E. ed. *The multi-problem dilemma.* Metuchen, N. J., Scarecrow Press, 1968.

Hollis, F. *Casework: A psychosocial therapy.* New York: Random House, 1964.

Richmond, M. *Social diagnosis.* New York: Russell Sage Foundation, 1922.

JAMES R. DUMPSON was twice the Commissioner of Social Service for New York City. In between his municipal appointments, he was Associate Dean of Hunter College School of Social Work and Dean of Fordham University School of Social Service.

Chapter 7

JAMES DUMPSON

Your reputation today is primarily as an administrator, and you may see yourself now totally as one. But I recall that in the 1950s, you had a lot to do with gangs and with setting up the Youth Board. I remember the youth gangs—the West Side Story bit—and, to my mind, Youth Board was a rather impressive clinical agency. How did you see it then?

Actually, my work with the gangs preceded the Youth Board. The so-called street workers came out of a project that I directed known as The Central Harlem Street Clubs Project. This was an attempt to find out how social workers reach out, relate to, and seek to effect and change behavioral patterns of the gang at that time.

What years are we talking about?

I'm now talking '49, '50, and '51. Out of that came the whole Youth Board activity of Jim McCarthy and Lillian Lampkin and a whole slew of other people. It's interesting that you identify the clinical aspect of my professional life.

In later years, particularly during my deanship at Fordham, I think I was perceived as just the opposite.

I'm sure you are now. But you must have started out in your long career in social work working with people.

That's correct. I started working in Pennsylvania. I went into the Pennsylvania Department of Public Assistance and worked as a social investigator. I was working with people on a family and individual basis, and then moved into supervision in that department. Then I came to New York as a caseworker in the Children's Aid Society, working with children who were being placed in foster care and, therefore, working with children, parents, and foster parents. That is 37 years ago.

Children's Aid Society is still in existence?

Very much in existence—the oldest child placement agency in the United States.

Like anyone who has been in social work for any length of time, you began by working with people and had to climb the ladder. Is it possible today to go right into administration or be a social worker and not work directly with people?

I think it might be possible. I would not recommend it. But, first of all, I don't think that one can define administration as other than working with people. And much of what I learned, let's say in the course of human growth and development—in those days we used to call it human growth and behavior—is the very essence of administration in a large sense, or of my perception of administration. As a matter of fact, that is the distinction I make between administration and managers. To me, managers in public administration are not concerned with relationship, and at the very core of administration is this concept of relationship that we talk so much about in social work. The difference I perceive, however, is the use of relationship. Obviously, with people who come to me for conferences, or with my relationship with staff (and there are 28,000), I'm not attempting to affect their behavior except insofar as it relates to the mission of the agency and getting a specific job done. This is a little different than where I was when I was a caseworker working with an adolescent child in Children's Aid Society, where the end goal was behavioral change on the part of that individiaul child and/or in his relationship to the parent, and the parent in relationship to the family, and the family's relationship, ultimately, to the community. Although I must admit, in those days we never got to that.

Here, I am concerned with relationships with individuals and groups in this agency and trying to understand some of the dynamics that go into effecting change, then into our systems change; but you can't talk about systems change unless you talk about people in the system—how they react to, how they respond to, how they perceive change, and what the administrator is all about; how I get them to like what I want done without having them necessarily like me, Jim Dumpson, as a person. All of this, you see, is why I believe an administrator should not come out of a school of social work, for example, and become commissioner of social services or the head of a foster home agency or administrator of a family agency. The experience of working with individuals and with groups and testing out one's skills and one's own perception of self in relation to other individuals and groups is terribly important.

I'll give an example. Last night, I was sitting here about half past six. One of my assistants came in here and said, "You can't go out yet. There's a demonstration downstairs." I said, "Who's demonstrating?" "About ten of our patrolmen are demonstrating." I said, "What are they demonstrating about?" "Well," she said, "they are charging harassment, etc." I said, "By whom?" "I really don't know." "Have they asked to see me?" She said, "No. They're just demonstrating." And I thought first: "Yes, I can go out. I can go out to the side door where the car comes and picks me up and avoid them. Or I can go out through the front door and deal possibly with a confrontation by ten men. Or"—and this one I selected—"I can invite a delegation of them to come up and tell me what it is all about."

Four of them came up. We spent an hour talking about their grievance. When it was all over, another assistant turned to me and said: "You know, you won't last very long if you see every group that demonstrates or that has a grievance." I said, "I don't know what you mean by 'lasting very long,' except that I won't last very long unless I do talk to people to get some sense of what's bugging them and what it is I can do about it, if anything. Show them my limitations as the commissioner. Tell them where the targets are, if they are outside of this agency, and so forth."

That, to me, is administration. It's dealing with people. It's working with people. It's communicating with people. It's sharing with people. You see, what came out of that was to help them to see where to find redress for what they wanted and to use the resources that they had failed to take account of. Well, you know, I had to live through helping a youngster or a mother or a family learn how to use himself or herself in relation to a total environment and to use resources before I knew how to help a group of angry patrolmen do the same thing. And what worried me after I got home was: Did I do the right thing? Did I co-opt them, because they were not angry when they left? When I did go downstairs to get in the car, about 15 of them were in a group and only one of them said anything to me: "Good night, Commissioner." And having lived through a strike in this department when other behavioral responses followed my emergence through that door, I worried a little bit last night about what I'd done. Had I been really helpful as commissioner? Or should I have let them demonstrate?

You have a lot of worries in this job. What's the biggest worry?

My biggest worry is whether I can pull off the expectations that my appointment has aroused among large sections of the staff. I represent to the staff a commitment to services. I therefore represent a difference between what my predecessor and what I represent. I talk about services, about staff qualifications, about training. I talk about clients as human beings. I'm afraid I have raised the expectations of large sectors of this staff that now we are going to be a service agency, and I'm not sure I can bring that about because of a lot of forces that I can't control.

At the American Public Welfare Association meeting in 1974, I gave a speech at the close of the conference. A woman from a regional office of the federal government came up and said: "I have one thing I have to say to you. Thank God services have come back to New York City." That just added to my worry because I'm not sure we can do it, even though I'm committed to it, I believe in it, and I don't think we have any reason for being unless we can do it.

Your immediate predecessor in HRA was a management man.

Jules Sugarman, who came after Jack Goldberg. And before Jack Goldberg came Mitch Ginsburg, and before Mitch Ginsburg came Jim Dumpson. Probably you're thinking of Arthur Spiegler and Charles Morris and that whole group of magical experts that came out of Harvard.

Well, Ginsburg, Goldberg, and yourself are rather distinguished social workers and educators. Ginsburg is dean of the Columbia School, Goldberg was Dean at New York University, and you at Fordham. That's a rather impressive, talented group of men, and yet you all seem to struggle with this job. You evidently took some time to regenerate; now you're back in the fray. I have two questions for you. What is it that made you leave academia and return to this very difficult struggle? And what is there about the job itself that seems to defy solution? Is it not solvable?

The first question: Why did I leave academia and come back to what I knew was here, since I had been here before? Most of my colleagues said they could understand a person going to that job who had not been there, but they could not understand my going, having been there.

Did anyone call you masochist?

That's right. And I did have a struggle. I had a wonderful relationship with a wonderful faculty at Fordham. I had a wonderful relationship with the student body and with the university generally. And, as a matter of fact, we had just finished our re-accreditation process, and it was very clear that the school was going to be accredited for another ten-year period. So educationally and professionally and administratively, everything was fine.

Why did I leave? What was the struggle? I left for a couple of reasons. I had been dean of that school for seven years and, before that, associate dean for two years at Hunter. I had helped reshape the curriculum of Fordham University Graduate School of Social Service. I had been the president of the Council of Social Work Education for about four years, and I had some input into the redirection of social work education, insofar as the council has that role. I thought the time had come to go back into practice and to test out what I had taught and had done in terms of revision as far as curriculum was concerned. In fact, I once said to my faculty that if I had my way in academia, every member of the faculty would go back into practice, whatever the setting, for a year before he came back to teach again. I would do that whether he was teaching social work practice or casework or whatever. So I wanted, first of all, to test out what I had been part of in the whole educational process of students coming into the profession and whether this had validity or not. And I am testing it out.

There is another reason—maybe more political. I chaired the Task Force on Social Welfare during Mayor Beame's campaign, and I made it very clear then that I was not doing it for political reasons. I belonged to no political club, I had never been in a club house in my life. But when the mayor asked me to do it, it seemed to be an opportunity to say to him in the Task Force report some things I thought he needed to hear. Whether he accepted them or not was his right. But there was a commitment that I could be free as chairman, and I could select the people, with one or two exceptions, and I would submit to him the report. He would do with it as he would, and I'd go back to Fordham and continue being dean.

After the election, Mayor Beame asked me if I would accept the position of commissioner, and I said, "No. Under no circumstance." He asked me again, and I said no. Other people began to ask me and I said no. And then there came, you remember, a blow-up about that time, and I said "Ok, I will do it." I will digress for a moment to say why I did say I would do it.

I thought: if Mayor Beame wants me that much and he has seen and studied that Task Force report, then maybe I have a good chance of beginning to turn the system around. I did not agree with where it was under the administration of Jules Sugarman, whom I know and admire as a person, but philosophically he and I are worlds apart—philosophically in terms of people, how people's needs should be met. So when the mayor kept pressing, and I knew who the alternatives were if I had finally said no, I thought of the challenge to test out and yet hold on in academia—I have an adjunct appointment at Fordham, and I'm going to teach one semester there. It was an opportunity to help the mayor and at least test out what I think the department should be. And his willingness to have me do it, and symbolically what I represented, I hope, professionally in the community. I said, "Ok, the problems are there, but maybe I can make a contribution, even if I only stay six months." It would have meant something to the staff who were there: some who have come through my school, some whom I know have come through other schools not dissimilar to mine, are committed to a certain value system that is part of the profession. What would it mean to them to have a dean of a graduate school of social work come back as commissioner and say: "This is what we stand for." So these were some of the pieces that went into my thinking.

It was also a struggle because financially the job meant very little. I did not go back to the pension system—maybe unwisely, as I look back, but that was a decision I made then —because I learned that if I went back into the pension system, I would have to commit myself to five years of service before I would have the benefit of all that has come into the pension system since I left in '65 and would be able to retire at half salary. But I decided that I didn't want to go back in the pension system because I didn't want a commitment of five years in public service. I wanted to be absolutely free of any fiscal or monetary considerations if I went back. And I wanted to be able to say to staff—as I had to say to them—"I didn't come back to earn my pension."

I'm not in the retirement system. I maintained the equity I had in it, but I am not a contributing member and therefore cannot benefit. There was some cynicism about that; some of the staff said: "He's come back to get his pension. He doesn't care about us. He doesn't care about the program. And as soon as he gets enough in, he's going to go."

Were you restless?

At school? I think that was a small part of it. I had said to the faculty that I didn't think that anyone should be dean of a school longer than five years. I always thought a dean should go in, make his contribution, add to the growth and development of the school, and move on and let somebody else come in and build on it. I was there seven years. I decided not to leave at the beginning of the sixth because re-accreditation was coming up. I had been quite a force in changing that curriculum, and I thought it would be irresponsible for me to go just before it was up for re-accreditation. (At that time, I wasn't thinking of coming here. Some other office was available.) I wanted to be there to defend, or help to defend, the educational experience we were providing for students and the rationale for it before the Commission on Accreditation. But I think at best I would have stayed at Fordham only one more year. You get very comfortable with faculty. You get very comfortable with the situation. People know you too well; you know them too well.

Would you like to take a crack at my larger question, which was not so much why you, Jim Dumpson, came in to struggle with this job, but what is there about this job that somehow seems to elude many talented men? What is there about being Commissioner of Welfare? Your predecessors weren't quite able to do what they wanted. Is the job too big? Is it too difficult? Is it beyond solution?

I think the present system is beyond solution. I think the most that a Mitch Ginsburg, a Jack Goldberg, or a Jim Dumpson, or anybody else like us who comes out of our background can do is patchwork. Patchwork that hopefully protects the client to the extent possible from damages that the system must inflict and that protects staff from the hurt and the damages that the system, as it is set up, must inflict. I can't speak for the others, but part of what made me come back was: Can I help a little bit, even though I don't believe that the system is viable for the present as a way of helping people who are in need. That's one part. The other is my total commitment and conviction that the basic structure for the delivery of services to people is fundamentally a public responsibility.

I talk a lot about complementarity, and by that I mean that the public, the government, has the ultimate responsibility of assuring the availability of services. That doesn't mean that government must deliver all the services. But it does have the responsibility of assuring the availability of all services, the quality of them, and the appropriateness of them, but with the voluntary sector complementing that. I reject, you see, the whole business of residualism, which is part of the New York scene. So again we come back when a mayor asks you to return. You don't believe in the system, but you might be able to change that residualism around to complementarity.

How would you define residualism?

By residualism I mean that government is the last instrumentality for serving people. One starts with one's family. If that isn't sufficient, one's immediate community. Then one goes to the Church and volunteerism and government as the last resort. And as I understand it, it used to be a fundamental tenet in the Catholic social service field that government was the residual and that sectarian organizations had primary responsibility, once one had to turn outside of one's own family for assistance. Even as a Catholic, I reject that—and rejected it when I was here before and will continue to reject it.

And the fight that came about when I came in, which incidentally was another piece of my coming, was my position on *Wilder* v. *Sugarman.* I thought: My God, if I can help from the inside, win the *Wilder* v. *Sugarman* suit, and assure availability of services to children who may need them— whether they're Catholic, Protestant, Jewish, black, white, green, or whatever—through public assumption of its primary responsibility even if I could do it only for a year or two.

You're talking now abut the suit against child care agencies because they are sectarian.

That's right, that's right. This is a class action suit brought in the federal court by the New York American Civil Liberties Union and the New York Legal Aid Society to challenge the constitutionality of the New York City foster care system. The system is rigidly organized along sectarian lines: Jewish, Catholic, and Protestant. The City of New York purchases foster care services from these sectarian agencies for close to 90 percent of all children who need care at public expense. The suit charges, further, that there is discrimination against black children, who are predominantly Protestant, by virtue of the priority given by each sectarian group to children of its own faith and the failure of the Protestant system, or inability of the Protestant system to provide adequate services for Protestant black children, resulting in their being denied appropriate services. The suit further challenges the right of the State and City of New York to purchase foster care services based on religion. Finally, the suit challenges the right to deny foster care services to those who are neither Protestant, Catholic, or Jewish.

Wilder is the family name of one of the children who was denied service because she was Protestant and black. Wilder is the name of the leading plaintiff in the class action. The defendants are Sugarman, State Commissioner Lavine, and the executives of all the voluntary child care agencies. Financial damages are sought from each of the defendants—hence *Wilder et al.* v. *Sugarman et al.* And I made a position statement that strongly supported the ALCU position that the child care agencies should not be sectarian.

I'm glad they had the suit. I happen to believe in sectarianism, but, more important, I believe in freedom of choice. If I need services, whether child care services or counseling for that matter, I ought to be free to go either to a Catholic agency because I'm Catholic or not go to a Catholic agency. But I ought to have some choice, and that choice includes availability of high-quality service under public auspices.

Let me ask you, Commissioner, along these lines: you must be familiar with the pairing of hospitals, which Dr. Ray Trussel instituted, whereby the public hospitals get paired with the voluntary. What are your thoughts on that? Have you ever thought of any such affiliating? And, if not, would it indicate that you prefer that public agencies improve themselves, more or less by their own bootstraps?

I support the hospital affiliation model because it has helped make it possible for the public or municipal hospital not to be perceived as hospital services for the poor, which really means poor-quality hospital care. It enriched the quality of care by virtue of making accessible the trained, expert personnel, already maldistributed in the voluntary hospital sector, to the municipal or public hospital system. As a result, we experienced improved, enriched hospital care for a wider spectrum of economic levels in the community.

I believe the hospital affiliation concept has much to contribute to the development of a high-quality social service system in New York. An affiliation or a cooperative public-voluntary agency relationship will bring similar benefits in the social service delivery sector. The expertise and unique know-how of the public and the voluntary sector are co-joined, and people are the beneficiaries.

My agency has just entered into a joint service-delivery project in the Chelsea area under the name of CAUSE. We have joined public agency staff with the Community Service Society staff in this project. Again, I believe the people in the Chelsea area are the primary beneficiaries. In addition, both the Community Service Society and the Department of Social Services will learn from each other and together in personal service provision. We may be developing one more module for the social service delivery system in New York, which must be attuned to the economic, racial, cultural, and religious variables that must be taken into account as we improve and extend social service provision in a city with so many ethnic, cultural, and economic differences. I intend to seek additional service affiliations with additional voluntary agencies as well as demonstrate, concurrently, service-delivery modules that involve only public agency personnel. In each instance, a program evaluation unit will be an integral part of the demonstration.

Isn't there a similarity here between the services available in the public agencies and hospitals versus the presumably better services available in the private?

Except that in the statement of admission that I have defined for the Human Resources Administration, that isn't so. The Social Security Act also does not exclude us; indeed, it mandates us to make services available to people who have other than financial need. It's never been accepted in the city and it's never been fully implemented in the state. But it says in the service provision of the Social Security Act that the public social services system shall make services available to people in need of services without regard to their financial position.

And I want to move this department to the place where, if you want to adopt a child, you don't have to be on public assistance to do it. If you can afford a fee, you can go to our adoption program and adopt a child there as well as from a private agency.

But what would the heads of private agencies think about that?

Well, the heads of the private agencies—if I may be very blunt with you—were very ambivalent about my return.

I understand they organized a couple of years ago to lobby their views.

That's right. For some parts of the program, they're delighted I'm here. They know I'm going to fight for clients' rights. They know I'm against the low grants we have. They know I'm going to seek staff. They know I'm for qualifications and standards and all the rest of it. But they also are very uncomfortable with my position about the role of the public agency vis-à-vis the role of the voluntary agency. And that was crystallized, you see, in the position I took on *Wilder* v. *Sugarman.* Sure, they would like to have Dumpson as head if he would just let the child welfare system alone.

What underlies this? Are we talking about attitudes towards poor? Are we talking about racism here?

We're talking about both. There's no question in my mind that we're talking about racism. There's no question that we're talking about selectivism from the point of view of the voluntary sector. We're talking about their wanting their cake and eating it too, and that gets reflected in racism —in racist policies and practices covered up by the concept of volunteerism: the right to do, to choose, and not to choose, but at the same time saying that they want to control that system. And they have controlled it. And they have controlled it, in my judgment, to the detriment of a large number of children. Not only those who are black or Puerto Rican but those who happen to be neither Catholic, Jewish, nor Protestant, because that's the way the pie is cut in this town. There are a large number of children in New York that are neither Jewish, Catholic, nor Protestant but have a right to services, whether child care services or family services or what have you.

I believe a sectarian agency has the right, with it's own funds, to give priority to people who are in the household of it's faith. I reject totally, however, that sectarianism shall be *the* system through which people get services and still have the right to give priority to people of their faith.

What's the position of the Catholic Church in this matter?

I'm in the Catholic Church, but I'm at odds with the Church on this. I'm at odds with the Jewish Federation on the *Wilder* v. *Sugarman* suit. I think, however, we're going to reach an accommodation because I am hell-bent on setting up—to the extent that I can command the money and the resources—a service system under public auspices that in some instances will purchase services from the voluntary sector, but purchase them on our terms, and that the accountability for what we purchase and the conditions under which we purchase and to whom they're available will be determined by the purchaser.

You see, what we now have is not a purchase system; we have a subsidy system. I don't know why this department, for example, should go out and set up a lot of new institutions for children when institutions are dotted all over the landscape under voluntary auspices. That's misuse of public funds. I see no reason why I shouldn't purchase from a residential treatment center if that residential treatment center is prepared to give its services to the child we determine to be in need of those services.

We'll contract. We'll pay so much a day. But you won't tell me, if you're the giver, that "Well yes, but we'll give preference to Catholic children or to Protestant children first and then we'll take yours." I would say, "No. I won't purchase on those grounds." Or if, by employing all the diagnostic skills, we can assess that a child is emotionally disturbed, and you have a program that meets the needs of this kind of child and he has an IQ of 40, and you say, "Yes, we'll take the children with IQs down to 40," then you can't reject that child and say "We aren't ready to take him yet," and give me all the reasons they give me for not taking him —not if I'm going to purchase services as a representative of the public.

Do you think you're going to win this suit?

I think we're going to win this suit. I think what's going to happen before this suit is over is that we're going to come to accommodations with the voluntary agencies.

Now I understand more about your first main worry. If you win this suit, you have an opening to do some very important things for the first time, strictly in the public domain. And then you've got to attract the people to do it.

And then you've got to have the money with which to do it.

You always felt that people should get back into practice. I've often felt that all trained social workers should give at least one year in public service because most professional social workers will not, if they get their degree, go to the Department of Welfare, where their skills are probably most needed. It becomes a matter of status. But you seem to want to do, in a way, what the Youth Board did back in the fifties as a public agency. It had such morale.

It had professional status.

It certainly did. People were fighting to get in.

No student who came out of Fordham during my seven years there had any question about where his or her dean stood in terms of that graduate's responsibility to the public sector. Indeed, when we redefined the mission of that school several years ago, I didn't endear myself to some of my faculty when I said to students that, "If you're coming here just to become commissioners or private practitioners, this is not the school for you. There are other schools; go there. This is not what we're about. If you're going to leave this school and go up into a nice quiet community in Westchester, that's not what we are here for, because contributing to the elimination of poverty is one of the education objectives of this school. That means working right in the ghettos, where the need is the greatest." I'm not saying that Westchester doesn't have need for social workers, they do.

You felt you had an urban school?

We *are* an urban school. We're training for the urban community, and that's why we reached out as hard as we did to bring in more minority students—Puerto Rican, particularly. We're an urban school, and the need is urban. That doesn't mean that some other school shouldn't train for Westchester practice, but not here.

You even sound like a much more service-oriented school. I've often wondered why all the schools of social work call themselves something different. Some are "social service" and some "social work" and some something else.

There's a reason for that. There are, I think, three or four schools of social service in the United States out of the 80-odd graduate schools of social work. All four of them are Catholic or have a Catholic background.

But there is something psychological about that.

Yes, there is something psychological about that. At one point, I was about to ask the trustees to change the name of Fordham Graduate School of Social Service and then decided against it. I didn't want any students of Fordham to get a feeling that there was something denegrating about service, or that being in the School of Social Service meant that they were any less than social workers professionally. Or that they had any less of the skills, the knowledge and understanding, and so forth of helping because we were a school of social service.

Who has been the most influential person or persons who has shaped your philosophy and attitudes?

You'd be surprised. One was a woman by the name of Dorothy C. Kahn. Dorothy Kahn was on the faculty of the Pennsylvania School of Social Work and she was director of the Philadelphia County Board of Public Assistance. Dorothy Kahn left that school and left that job—indeed she was kicked out so they could bring in a businessman to run public welfare in Philadelphia. She came to New York and went first to the refugee program and finally ended up at the United Nations. Dorothy was a personal friend and a teacher. It was she who got me into international social work. She was wonderful.

Another was a woman, a professor now dead, Rosa Wessel, whose writings you may know about. Rosa Wessel was a professor and taught casework at the Pennsylvania school. I still cherish the notes she wrote on the papers I wrote in her classes. I frequently quote what she once said to me. I'll never forget it if I live to be 150 years old; it's a very simple statement but a very meaningful one. I handed in a paper late and I said to her: "Mrs. Wessel, I'm sorry that this paper's late but I really didn't have time." She looked at me and in typical functional language said: "Mr. Dumpson, you have all the time that there is." I've never forgotten that, and I've repeated it to students and everybody else.

A third person was a woman who had been in the public welfare department in Philadelphia when I was there. Sarah Marnell was what we would call a welfare center director. She brought me to New York when she left that department and came to the Children's Aid Society to be case supervisor for a demonstration project that the society was doing in 1940 known as the Service Bureau for Colored Children. The demonstration project was financed by foundations to demonstrate that foster homes could be found for black children in New York City. The project was incorporated into the Children's Aid Society, and that's when I stayed on. Sarah Marnell had public welfare experience, she had been in the Jewish Family Agency in Philadelphia, she had been a part-time member of the faculty at Pennsylvania School. She was my immediate supervisor when I came to Children's Aid, and she turned out later to be a life-long friend until she died.

The fourth and last person, I guess, was Dr. Leslie Pinckney Hill, a man who had nothing to do with social work at all. He was the president of the State Teachers' College at Cheyney, Pennsylvania, where I went before I even thought of social work. He was black. He had been a close associate of Booker T. Washington in Hampton, and he came to Cheyney as the president. I went to Cheyney because I was too poor to go any other place when I graduated high school. Dr. Hill was a great man, and what he gave me was something that I had never had in my early development. I had always gone to integrated schools in Philadelphia. In fact, in the early years of my life, I went to a Quaker school and then into the public schools, and they were integrated. I knew nothing at all about what we now refer to as the black perspective or black culture. I just knew nothing until I went to Cheyney.

Where is Cheyney?

In Pennsylvania, and it was a school started back in 1737 by the Quakers. It used to be called The Institute for Colored Youth before slavery was ended, and then it moved into the State Normal School structure in Pennsylvania. It became one of the state teachers' colleges. When I was there, it was 99 percent black, faculty and students.

Did you grow up in Pennsylvania?

Yes, in Philadelphia.

In integrated areas?

Yes. I went to Temple University for one semester, but I couldn't afford to stay. My parents were very poor. Cheyney was a state school and I could afford to go there.

So you can't say that you were in advance of black perspective?

Not at all. I acquired it by accident. But at Cheyney I came to know about Negro spirituals. I had a wonderful art teacher, Laura Wheeler Waring, who I later learned was one of the great artists of our country. I liked music and I liked the creative arts, and I developed a relationship with Mrs. Waring and with Dr. Hill because I played the piano and, later, the organ at the school. I learned a whole new culture. I learned about black writers. I never had heard of people like W. E. B. DuBois, for example. I hardly had heard of Paul Robeson, even though we were almost contemporaries.

In high school, maybe another influential person was a man by the name of Dr. Burke, who taught Shakespeare. I was in a real minority group. In a class of 400, there were five blacks who graduated. And I remember Dr. Burke saying to me one day in class: "Did you ever hear of Dr. Alain Leroy Locke? I want you to find out who he is and come back and tell us in class." That was when I found out that Alain Leroy Locke was the first black Rhodes Scholar in the United States and that Dr. Burke had been his teacher in Central High School in Philadelphia. I came to know Dr. Locke later on in my life. But these are people who wove different things into my life.

What led you to social work?

Dissatisfaction with teaching. I taught for three years in a segregated school outside of Philadelphia known as Oxford, and I was the head teacher in a three-room elementary school. I had three or four classes in one room. There was a beautiful school one block away which was the elementary, junior, and senior high school for white students in Oxford. Oxford is just north of the Mason-Dixon line, as you cross from Maryland into Pennsylvania. It had all of the earmarks of that area. I just felt that there was nothing there for me to do. I couldn't get close enough to the children. I couldn't get close enough to the families. The school structure didn't permit it. I knew that I wanted to do something that wasn't there for me to do. Then I went into the public welfare department and from public welfare into social work.

You really had been exposed to both integrated and segregated experiences, and from the way you speak about your college, you sound like it was quite good for you.

The segregated college was a positive experience. One I wouldn't give a million dollars for because I had gone, you see, to an integrated elementary school. I had gone to a predominantly white high school. Cheyney was very enriching for me. I never saw a black teacher beyond the fourth grade until I got to the State Teachers' College because there were no black high school teachers in the West Philadelphia High School for Boys. So it was an enriching experience for me and had a great impact on my developing a healthy sense of identity.

I don't know what kind of sick person I would have ended up being had I gone on to a white college and taken a bachelor's and a master's and what have you and still have never seen as role models people who were other than white. And then getting into all the activities that I've been into professionally—the ease with which I could have become isolated or alienated from my own ethnic group.

I've often thought of the days and weeks and even months that I've sat around the table in a leadership role, and the only people around that table were white. How easy it would have been to have forgotten that I live in the United States and there is such a thing as black, white, and brown and all the rest of it.

But to cap it all off, going to Africa this summer was an experience that moved me more deeply and more keenly than I expected a trip to move me. I went to Ethiopia and then to Ghana, to Sierra Leone, to Kenya, and then to Senegal. I was tour leader for an ICSW [International Conference on Social Welfare] group, and that was an experience for me. It was more than just sightseeing; it was an emotional experience that I was not prepared for. They showed all of us, not just me, where the slaves came from in that area, where they went and how they went. And then when I went to Dakar and saw what they preserved there, I had to deal with some feelings that I hadn't been prepared to deal with. I was a leader of a group of 34 people. Half of them were black and the other half were white, and for the second time in my life, I felt I had to deal with hostile feelings against others who were not black. (The first time was the first time I went to Europe.) But I was quite conscious of what was happening to me.

Except you were not in a minority.

But that didn't compensate for what I was living. Afterwards, I was able to talk about it to some of the group, some of the whites that night over drinks. I was surprised and I suppose, in a way, supported by their sharing with me what their feelings were. They weren't too different from mine, and that was surprising. They were perceiving it differently; they were feeling a sense of guilt. We all agreed they didn't need to feel guilty nor did I need to feel hostile, because none of us were actors in what we were witnessing. We were able to sit around and talk about it. I remember the experience very well. I'll never forget it.

Would you like to speculate on where social work is going? You must have given a great deal of thought to the whole issue of professionalism.

I'm worried about social work as a profession. I'm worried about it because we seem to be dividing ourselves into camps, and I think that the splintering is going to weaken what it is that is uniquely ours as a profession. And for a profession that says it can recognize difference and deal with difference, professionally we seem not able to do so.

Let me give some examples of what I'm talking about. When I was dean at Fordham, both the Society of Clinical Social Workers and Clark Blackburn of the Family Service Society of America sent some rather sharp letters to me and to all deans about what they perceived to be our weaknesses as educators and how we had abandoned preparation for clinical practice. We were going all the way over to the other side and so forth and so on. I said to Clark once: "It's not either/or; there is a need in our profession for clinicians. There is a need in our profession for what I'd like to think of as people able to deal with micro and macro systems. I don't know why we have to say that everybody has to be this or everybody has to be that. Part of our weakness is that we have all been too long in one mold. And I don't know why clinical social workers or private practitioners or community organizers have to separate themselves into warring camps, so to speak, and have intraprofessional fights. I'm worried because, while we're doing that, I'm afraid some newly formed, newly perceived, newly conceived professional groups will move in and say "This is ours, this is ours" and split our professional center. That's one example.

Secondly, I'm worried about the profession from one angle that I hope is temporary, and that is the divisions that are occurring along ethnic and cultural lines—National Association of Black Social Workers, National Association of

Puerto Rican Social Workers, National Association of Chicanos, Mexican Americans. The black students came to me in school and said, "We want a course on social work practice with blacks," and I said, "What is that? You have to define it for me. Are you telling me there are certain skills and knowledge you have to have to work with blacks that's different than working with another person with a problem? And if it is, and I'm not saying it isn't, hadn't we better do some research and identify what those skills are? Because I can't set up a course unless I'm sure that I've got faculty who can teach that difference."

What are the differences? It may be attitude. It may be a lot of other things. But I'm not sure that the skills required to work with the family aren't the skills required to work with the black family. And the social worker really has flexibility in the use of those skills, including the cultural component. So I worry about that.

And finally, I'm worried about the profession organizationally represented by NASW. I hear, and I hope I'm wrong, that our strength and our validity as a profession is going to come from bigness. We flaunt the fact that we have 78,000 members of NASW and so forth. I don't care whether we have 78,000 or 7,800 if we aren't doing something to change the impact of the economic system on people and not get ourselves so tied up with organizational structure and membership drives.

Are you worried about professional standards?

I'm worried about professional standards only to the extent that they may be so rigidly defined as to exclude people who might well be included. That takes me to another subject that you shouldn't have brought up. It isn't new—you've heard it before and I hope you will agree with it.

There are levels of skill required for different kinds of tasks. I would hope that the profession could embrace a much wider spectrum of tasks dealing with the helping of people and therefore embrace a much wider range of skill levels to be developed. That's why I'm very hep on, for example, the undergraduate program, as I am of the other end of the doctoral program, whether it's for clinical program or what have you. But I see the issue there as one of standards—establishing standards for performance that relate to the tasks that are to be performed for different client groups at different points in time. The case aide, the paraprofessional, to me needs to be embraced by our profession. They're dealing with people. They're helping people. And I can see all kinds of classes of "professionals," if you will. But I'm worried about professionalism that becomes exclusive and that denies any kind of credential to the person who doesn't have an MSW. I don't need all MSWs in my service programs department. But, by God, I do need people who have the value stance, the value posture of the profession, and are willing to commit themselves to the code of ethics that is the hallmark of our profession. What they do and the skills and knowledge they need to do it can be differentially defined. That's one reason I was against the licensing bill. It excluded too many groups that ought to have been included and whom we ought to be supervising and training and "controlling" in a sense.

Perhaps you have, from your position, much more of an understanding of the whole concept of service as economics—as employability in what will probably be one of the major areas of employment in this country in time, if it isn't already there.

I view the availability of a broad spectrum of personal or social services (Al Kahn refers to them as social utilities) as essential for all people in our highly industrialized, technological society without reference to economic strata—services that are readily accessible and universally available. I believe there are several economic considerations to my position. First, the demand for trained social service personnel can only increase, notwithstanding the seeming or actual shift of the federal administration away from the need for social services and training of personnel to provide them. Further, the economic development of every nation is inextricably linked to the level of social development achieved, and optimum social development depends on the availability of a variety of social supports. Economic and social development, I am convinced, are inseparably linked—to neglect one is to adversely affect the other.

I once stated in a speech that the quality of life in a community, in a city, in a nation cannot be divided among various sectors of the population. An acceptable quality of life must be assured for all individuals, families, and groups. To achieve this will require a greater allocation of our material resources as a nation to assure the availability of the numbers and various levels of skilled persons needed. We could drastically reduce our unemployment situation nationally and increase markedly our national productivity if we looked to and assured the manpower needs of the personal service system. Of course, we would still have the task of assuring an equitable distribution of the opportunities and fruits of that productivity, but we would have made a quantum leap as a nation toward achieving the general welfare.

SELMA FRAIBERG is Professor of Child Psychoanalysis at the University of Michigan, Ann Arbor. In 1959 she wrote *The Magic Years,* now a classic which has been translated into many languages.

Chapter 8

SELMA FRAIBERG

First let me ask you: Why social work? What led you to choose this field?

I came from a family in which philanthropic commitment was very important. Members of our family were prominent in Jewish community welfare organizations and philanthropic organizations. So I grew up with a tradition that was very easily adapted to the profession of social work.

Are you the first professional to move in the direction of social work in your family?

I was the first in my generation. My father was a businessman, and members of my family were board members and active in community fund raising. I always knew what they were raising funds for, and I always knew enough about agencies so that I heard about the field even before I knew very much about it. We were a very close family, and so we all spoke of these things; it was a very natural thing. There was a tradition of Jewish philanthropy that was very

deeply felt and not limited to raising money. In my home
there was discussion of the aged, the orphans. I remember
the impoverished Jewish families of the Depression. Jewish
families were not any more impoverished than anyone else,
of course, but in Jewish tradition, one had to especially care
that the members of the tribe may be imperiled. So all that
was available to me; I think I was the only one who chose
social work.

How many of you were there?

In my own family, there was a brother who is a physi-
cist, he's next.

You're the oldest?

Yes, I'm the oldest—and a sister who is a teacher. And
then in the larger family, the cousins distribute themselves
over many professions: medicine, law, engineering, profes-
sorial appointments in English, history, etc.

*Does that core of professionalism among you and your cousins
come from a long professional orientation in your family, or is this
more in your own generation?*

No, I would say that in my mother's family, the college
members would be two or three. In my own generation, in
the extended family there was only one who did not go to
college.

At the time I came into social work in the early forties,
it was the most exciting profession for a young woman. And
since everyone in my generation was very much affected by
the Depression or the War and by a commitment to actively
participate in reshaping the world, social work was really
the natural choice.

After graduating, I started out in public assistance in
the early days of ADC [Aid to Dependent Children] without
any certainty that I would go on to graduate school. I had
one year that I consider one of the most valuable years of
my life in ADC. Got a sense of the complexity of human
problems—the effects of poverty and the broken family
upon children. I learned a good deal about interviewing

and listening and I had good supervision, and it soon became apparent that if I wanted to be a social worker, I would have to go to graduate school, which I did. I entered the School of Social Work at Wayne State in 1941—a particularly auspicious time. And very luckily, (and all of this *was* luck because so much depends on your supervisor, as you know) I got a first-rate, most admirable supervisor, Miss Clarice Freud. She remains my friend and is a consultant to our own program here.

This was in a child placement agency, which I think threw me into the depths of human problems. It was very painful for a young social worker to see children removed from their own homes. It was even more painful because of the fact that this was the time that Hitler's refugee children began to come over, and we were responsible for the placement of that group of children.

I wasn't sure I could survive in social work now that I really understood how much suffering one would have to share with patients, and small children especially. And it was only, I think, through the steadiness of a supervisor who allowed me to feel but also showed me the necessity of containing my feelings so that I could be truly helpful to my children that I stayed in social work at all.

Thereafter, I had a second year in a family agency, again with great supervision, and I think my whole story would have been different if I had not had first-rate supervisors and first-rate training. Again, I had a caseload of impoverished families mainly. I learned the methods of social work—methods of social treatment for a wide variety of families with a wide range of problems. I also carried direct treatment cases with children under supervision and again had the feeling of how little I knew and of how much I would have to know.

During one period of training, I was also an initiator with Fritz Redl of early group work on behalf of children. We set up a series of what would now be called group

treatment programs for children who were in our placement caseload at the Jewish Children's Bureau. And I was
very much fascinated with the potential in group treatment
for certain disorders of childhood. I think I also saw the
limitations. I made a decision, finally, that I was best suited
for casework. But I needed more analytic supervision.

And then there was a period of time in which I had a
mixture of experiences. The Veteran's Administration
opened its mental health clinic in the early post-war years,
and I spent a year working in the V.A. clinic with adults.
Found that very rewarding in many ways. But I did not get
the psychiatric supervision that I had hoped for. It was
really the early chaotic, formative period of the V.A. And
in the meantime, something happened that led me into
analytic work. I had been carrying some cases under analytic supervision in both my field placements.

*Was that a matter of routine at Wayne State, or was this also
just good juck?*

You know, it wasn't a matter of luck. Nearly every
major agency at that time had an analytic consultant. Usually, by the way, they were the best men and women available, so I had good teachers. Then, because there were very
few child therapists and my work was known to some of my
supervisors, I began to get child patients, which I carried
under analytic supervision. And in a way I can't really describe, I moved more and more into child treatment, always
with analytic supervision. I had available to me two excellent seminars conducted by the Sterbas: one on psychoanalytic training and one in child therapy. And from
that point on, without consciously making a decision, I
moved in the direction of psychoanalysis.

In those days there were no formal training programs.
In fact, to this day, there are no formal training programs
for non-medical analysts.

Cleveland is the only place?

Cleveland and Chicago.

Well, during those years when I was an analyst, I was also a social worker in that I maintained close ties with social work. My social work colleagues almost insured that I would.

How did they do that?

Ara Cary, the director of the Downriver Consultation Service, asked me to do consultation work. I led a seminar there, and I never really lost touch with social work during those years. I didn't really want to either. I also did a fair amount of institute work in connection with a variety of social work organizations, and this was probably an important reason that I never lost touch with my own base in social work. I never completely became only a child analyst, seeing children in an office or seeing only a certain class.

You have never done that?

I have always done teaching, consultation, and supervision. I don't think there's ever been a time that I wasn't involved with social work. After our daughter Lisa was adopted—I became a rather late mother; she's now 18 and about to enter the University of Michigan—there was a period of time when I did very little work, naturally. It also coincided with the period that we moved to New Orleans. My husband has his doctorate in English and was on faculty, and during that period I had very limited time to work professionally, with my daughter still a preschooler. I taught one class in the School of Social Work at Tulane, and Viola Weiss was instrumental in bringing me in as consultant and seminar leader for her family agency. So once again, I was close to social work. I had almost no analytic practice but maintained connections with the New Orleans Psychoanalytic Institute, where I also taught a course occasionally. Then we moved back north, as we say; my husband became chairman of the Department of English at the University of Toledo. My daughter was then in third grade. There was a little bit more time, and I was invited to commute to Ann Arbor to teach for the Department of Psychiatry at the University of Michigan one day a week.

So for three years I gave something like one or two days a week there, and at the end of that three-year period, we moved to Ann Arbor, which has always been "home town," in a sense, for us. We were moving back to old connections and associations, and almost at the same time, my research in the development of blind infants was to be supported through grants.

Actually, the research began in New Orleans during the period that I was a full-time mother and had time to give freely to a very tiny investigation. We'd better move back there.

While I was consultant to the Family Service Society of New Orleans, the agency took on a caseload of blind children who had formerly been loosely grouped in a preschool program which had closed and now had no facility. It soon became clear that these families and children needed continuous family casework on behalf of the child. And for the first time, I saw blind children and disorders that I had *never* seen, except in the most severely disturbed sighted children. I found that I had nothing to offer our social workers as consultant to the program because I knew nothing about blindness and I knew nothing about the bizarre characteristics that I saw in these latency-aged children.

Autistic-like symptoms?

Yes. This same agency had seen one autistic sighted child in two years before the blind caseload appeared. David Freedman, who was another consultant and both a neurologist and psychoanalyst, had exactly the same impression as I: at least one-quarter of those blind children were autistic, and nearly all the others showed autistic patterns to varying degrees.

So Dave and I, both friends and colleagues, had inferred from the characteristics of latency children and preschool children that something had gone awry in the sensorimotor period in the first 18 months of life. And if we knew *what* the developmental impediments had been, we would probably be able to evolve a treatment program and have valuable information as well.

Our first step was to go to the library and find out what was known about the development of blind children from a psychological point of view. There was nothing. Nobody had ever conducted a developmental study on blind children. Then we decided to conduct our own study. There was no money. Naturally that didn't matter. I had time. We decided that the first baby that came to the attention of our agency who was blind but otherwise intact would be looked upon as a potential candidate, and we would try to enlist the cooperation of the parents in helping us understand the development of blind infants.

The first baby, Toni, arrived after a period of 5½ months—a black child whose blindness was caused, in a horrible irony, by the carelessness of a nurse who failed to administer silver nitrate so that Toni contracted opthalmia neonatorum—an otherwise beautiful child with a very devoted mother. David and I arranged to visit monthly, with the mother's very earnest cooperation. We borrowed a camera from the man next door, and we divvied up the film and processing bill each month. Kept very careful notes. And in about seven months, the one baby had already begun to inform us about the unique developmental patterns of blind infants.

We saw where the roadblocks came in. We saw the extraordinary problems for the mother in caring for the blind infant. And we also saw that a mother, otherwise adequate with four other children, was thrown into disorder, for all her good maternal feelings, by the strange developmental patterns of the blind child.

That meant we had some beginning insight, and we followed Toni for about 2½ years. Although we looked for other babies, no otherwise adequate ones came to our attention. But by the end of our work with Toni, it was easy to conceive of a treatment program that would be based upon what we had learned. At the close of that period my husband got the job that took us to Toledo, and David Freedman at the same time got a job at Baylor. But both of us independently have been engaged in research in infant development since.

When I came to Ann Arbor, I had the chance to do a little bit more, since one young resident in psychiatry, Dr. Barry Siegel, was interested in working with me. We also got a collaborator in psychology lent to us by the Department of Pediatrics, Dr. Ralph Gibson. We had the cooperation of our opthalmology department and began pilot work in very well-defined research. Within about two years we had support from the National Institute of Child Health and Development for a larger program. At that time, we made it clear to NICHD that because these babies were at very great risk, we would need to offer *concurrent* educational counseling and guidance.

So it was a service as well as a research project?

Right. Our staff at that time was composed of clinical psychologists and social workers. And in addition to the research program, which was massive (we're still in the final data evaluation phase), we also had to work out educational and counseling approaches to the parents, knowing that they had not come to us as patients with neuroses but as parents faced with extraordinary problems in rearing a blind child. During the next years, we also began to get support from the Office of Education's Bureau of Handicapped Children, and we developed methods for a home-based education and guidance program on behalf of impaired infants. It was highly effective and made use of all the knowledge that the four disciplines could bring together: psychoanalysis, psychiatry, social work, and psychology. No part of the program could have been developed if we hadn't had all the disciplines involved.

We didn't do it, by the way, by dividing up chores. We all did the same work on the program. We all collaborated in developing the methods and brought in our special skills from our own areas—a model that we liked so well that it became the model for the current program here.

It was really your original interest, though, coming from New Orleans with the experience you had with Toni, that led to this. You have really generated this project?

Yes, I think I did. But I would draw attention to the fact that it came out of a clinical concern. I couldn't help the social workers in New Orleans. I couldn't help the parents. Part of this story is told in a paper [The Muse in the Kitchen, 1970] that I once presented at Smith College. It describes more fully how hypotheses are generated in a clinical setting and how they were examined in the research program and then brought back to the clinic and to the children.

In the interval between 1971 and 1973, we became strongly committed as a team to early intervention: we didn't have to be sold any longer on the benefits of early intervention. As a matter of fact, our own study revealed that our primary sample, in which all the blind children received educational guidance from the point of *referral* (often very early in the first year) came closer to sighted-child norms on standard tests than to blind-child norms. That includes language and motor development. The characteristic developmental lags were not present in our group taken as a whole. And "blindisms" also were rare occurrences or phased out appropriately at the end of the sensorimotor period. So that looking at our children (and we have some lovely tapes and films), one is startled by the fact that they don't *look* blind—until one realizes that the eyes are not making contact, the object is not being fixated. But they're otherwise adequate. We may find out more in the follow-up study, but the older ones are in school and with two exceptions are functioning very well.

How large were your samples in these groups?

In the restricted research sample, we have criteria that could be met only by a very small sample: ten. These were children who had no other handicaps, they were neurologically intact, and they were referred during the first year, as close as possible to the first trimester. We traveled within a radius of about 50 miles to get these children.

In another sample, however, we offered an educational program to children who were referred but who could not meet the criteria, and even some of these children who had known brain damage and other handicaps showed demonstrable differences in their attainments, compared to those in the general blind population who have had no intervention. All this remains to be more fully worked up, but a good part of the Group I material has either been published or will be ready for publication in a volume which will probably appear within the next year.

Are you writing it?

Yes, with collaborators. Volume I is nearly finished. And if I could just find time to complete one last chapter on language, then the book will be ready.

Now, to return to the new program. Since we did not need to be convinced (as if we ever did need to be) about the benefits of early intervention, we decided we would like to move into still another area which drew a lot of our concerns as clinicians and researchers. We already knew that many of the most severe and intractable emotional disturbances identified from children's clinics and hospitals often have their roots in the sensorimotor period and can be identified by trained clinicians *during* that period. Also, we have learned so much in the last decade, not only in our own research but in all areas of developmental psychology, about both the affective and the cognitive characteristics and milestones of the first two years of life that we should surely be able to translate this into early identification if we are good clinicians. And if we are good clinicians and understand those phases of development and treatment measures, then we should be able to translate our knowledge into effective treatment programs on behalf of the baby.

We call this an infant mental health program, and we applied for and received funds from the Grant Foundation for a pilot program for the first two years. We have just gotten renewal for another three years and an additional four-year grant from NIMH.

Has your interest in research and your scientific approach to the clinical situation and to what you see in practice, always been characteristic of your work, or is it something you developed? Do you see a dichotomy between the research and the clinical interest?

No, not at all. I have always argued closely for the intimate relationship between the clinician and the clinical researcher. You have to do *both*. Something has to be said for one's undergraduate experience too. Because, oddly enough, one never knows what one pulls out of one's basket of mixed blessings in an undergraduate curriculum. I was a psychology major and I had some training in experimental psychology, at least on an elementary level, and in perceptual psychology, which in my day in the late thirties and early forties was an utter bore. I hated every minute of it. I did well in it. I think I could have had a career in it, except that it was so detached from the human center that I could not see a career for myself in it. However, what came out of that was a background and a vocabulary and a theoretical framework that could be pulled out of the cellar, as it were, when I moved into the work with blind infants. So oddly enough, the years in the experimental lab with canned experiments, which I had thought an utter waste of time, could come back to me. Even though sensory and perceptual psychology has been very greatly modified today, nonetheless I was not without a vocabulary in the field or a way of approaching the problem. Furthermore, I had learned whatever it is that one gives to undergraduates: observational methods, rigor, methods for examination of a problem, how to *get* the answers.

It is very difficult to see how these factors come into clinical research because clinical research borrows quite another method. I think, as a matter of fact, it has moved too far away from our base in naturalistic study. We simply haven't exploited fully the naturalistic circumstances available to us or the clinical opportunity for generating hypotheses.

I think I've always moved back and forth between research and the clinic.

Always with a firm social work identification?

Yes. *And* with a firm psychoanalytic identification.

Are you upset or concerned at all about the current angst of attack on clinical work in social work?

I'm depressed by it rather than angered. First of all, I can't imagine a clinician doing psychotherapy without making use of the greatest discoveries of our time. I lament the fact that our training in social work has badly christened all of us, so to speak. I think the analogy came to mind because of the joke about Christianity: "Has Christianity failed?" "No, it's never been tried." Psychoanalysis too and it's implications for social work practice have never really been explored fully or understood fully. So at the time it was abandoned—and I think it really has been abandoned by most schools of social work—we had not even given ourselves the time it would take to fully develop a method. And we have moved in our history as social workers from one fad to another without fully testing it, without fully appreciating it. Whatever was in vogue was borrowed pragmatically: it worked or it didn't work, it was integrated or it was not integrated, on a simple pragmatic basis and on a very shallow level. So now we find ourselves with a smorgasbord which has no common theory, and which cannot be taught as a body of knowledge any longer either.

At the same time, the gap between what is being taught in social work and what is needed in the field is so large that one finds oneself helpless before the task of finding qualified clinicians. In this department of ours and in our hospital, where social workers are being required to do psychotherapy, there is often nothing in their background that prepares them for this work. At a time when we know more about prevention of emotional disorders in childhood than we have ever known in the history of mankind, the sum total of the information available on child development to a graduate of a school of social work will be a two-hour-a-week course for 16 weeks, cradle to the grave. And early childhood will be one one or two lectures.

So when we bring social workers into our program, they are students; we have to build in the most intensive intramural seminar and didactic program, and supervision, to bring about beginning adequacy at the close of the year (we insist on a year). Any new social worker coming to our program is selected on the basis of expertness in his field in practice, someone who has already obtained some clinical skills, and *we* build in the child part. There's a protected caseload for the first year.

Do you think it's disinterest or hostility on the part of the schools toward psychoanalytic theory and its usefulness in a clinical setting?

I think in many schools they really believe it is not useful. But always there's a mixed faculty: there are members of our faculty who would consider the theory irrelevant and some who would not. That's true of every school I know, as a matter of fact—except Smith, which I think is still strongly committed to an analytic approach.

But of course I won't blame our field entirely for that either. I think psychoanalysis has not provided teachers in graduate schools, and I have been fascinated to see that in Boston, for example, where there is a strong analytic tradition in social work, it may very well be because the Bibrings and the Deutschs and distinguished senior psychoanalysts, many on the institute faculty, devoted themselves to teaching social workers. It is a very important teaching function for analysts. Smith and Case–Western Reserve might be exceptions, but in nearly every other school that I know, the teaching of "dynamic psychiatry" is given to the most talented resident of the year who is just about one step ahead of his class, if he's done his homework.

One needed great teachers to teach psychoanalysis, which is a very difficult body of knowledge to impart in a lecture series anyway. But with extraordinary gifts and with a sequence of courses in a two-year curriculum, one can build an appreciation of its complexity and its value. That is simply not done. It is a very demanding theory to master. It's hard work. It is not hard work, however, to grasp a gold-star reward system. That's easy. And I'm ashamed for those who have brought that into the curriculum because it's so easy to teach, and at a point, by the way, when its therapeutic efficacy has not been demonstrated as being better than any other method.

One would think that if social work is applied science, one would have gone to some trouble, before shifting the course of the ship, to examine the new bearing. We did the same thing with family group therapy. After about a decade of outcome studies which did not favor this method over other methods and cast some serious doubt about its value, social work embraced it.

Let me ask you about your own life. What do you do to relax? What do you do for fun?

Oh, gardening, family fun, reading. We're all great readers in our family.

What do you like to read most?

I like nineteenth century novels very much. I must confess I like them more than the experimental "examination of the interior" novel that is assaulting us today, although I do like a number of contemporary novelists: Saul Bellow, Solzhenitsyn. I read a very large amount of biography, autobiography, history. But mainly I think I relax with my favorite old-fashioned novels of character.

Time and again, I'm struck by how well literature has served people in our field in developing and maintaining their interests.

Oh yes, and also as one's first introduction before psychology to *imaginary* psychology.I think that one benefit must have accrued to all of us through reading: the refinement of our interest in the outward manifestations of character, the surface of character, which is especially well drawn by the nineteenth century novelist. And it's this attention to behavior and manners that always becomes a corrective to the passion for the interior that is part of our work too, you know.

If you were going on a long trip and could take with you only a few books, what would you take?

War and Peace! As a matter of fact, *War and Peace* actually was the direct cause of a cervical disc problem I developed in Mexico. I was reading it and was absorbed (as if I didn't know how the story would end), and I got into the most idiotic posture in one of those old-fashioned beds with old-fashioned pillows in Cuernavaca and began to experience some neck pain, but I couldn't put down the book. The pain became very severe, but I still couldn't put down the book. The next day I woke up quite incapacitated and very shortly afterward learned that I had a ruptured disc. I suffered from it after for some length of time, which I think is the greatest tribute I could give any novelist!

All right, let's see. Dostoevski; I'm very fond of the Russian novelists. I would take with me *The Brothers Karamazov* and *Crime and Punishment. The Possessed* wearied me; I don't think I would take that. Anyway, for relaxation one hardly needs *The Possessed* when one is in our field. *The Red and the Black* by Stendahl. And Dickens, and I don't know that I would care; I would pick *any* one off the shelf.

Thomas Mann. I have read just about everything of his. I would particularly take the Joseph stories with me and *The Magic Mountain*. And Gide's *The Counterfeiters*. . .

I see I can't limit you to only a few books.

Oh, I'm past that already, aren't I? I don't think I should be limited; I don't think that's fair.

Do you stay active in professional circles?

I still do a fair amount of lecturing, let's say a few times a year—and I do institutes in the area of development psychology. I am really as deeply committed to other disciplines as well as psychoanalysis, but I would say that most of my teaching and lecturing has been done within psychoanalysis. I am not active in any organizations. I am in no way active in my own department here at Ann Arbor. I do not attend faculty meetings; I'm on no committees. I decided I had no talent for that sort of thing. And no ambitions either. My time is better spent where I have some degree of competence. It's a matter of assessing in your old age: "What do I really have to contribute?"

You say "in your old age." Do they have here one of those mandatory retirement arrangements? And what would be the first thing you would do if you were forced to retire?

Oh, this would be no tragedy at all! If I were made to retire. . . Really I would hate to give up the work I am doing now, which is a great joy. But this work would really have to be carried on by younger people, so I think it would be very wise of me to retire as director of this project, let's say in five years or less, so that other people who are gifted —and I have many gifted people working for me—can take over and give the program continuity and life. At that time I would enjoy part-time teaching, a very limited private practice, and writing, writing, writing. I will not be able to finish some of the stuff I have been waiting to write up if I had 40 more years.

Is it easy for you to write? Can you just sit down and do it?

It's such a mundane method that I never wanted to

admit to anyone how I do it, until I discovered that most writers use the same method. I regularly sit down at a typewriter for an hour and a half every day whether I'm stuck in a paragraph or not. I just sit down. I regularly finish one or two pages a day. And while that sounds like a sleazy way of writing, I discovered to my very great satisfaction that Thomas Mann regularly wrote 40 lines a day and that a number of other writers, novelists among them and poets, did the same thing: so much work a day. If you wait for the inspiration to come, of course, it can either be there or not be there. But if the task is before you, you finally pick up the continuity, and it's that kind of continuity that produces the paper or the book.

You fuse your writing so beautifully with personal touches and real people. Is it a conscious attempt on your part, or is it just something that comes to you? I recently gave your book The Magic Years *to a friend, and I told her, "Don't miss the episode of 'Laughing Tiger.'" It is made so funny and so personal with anecdote and names and interchange. Do you do that on purpose to make it more rich for the reader?*

I do it for myself too, because if I can't make it rich for myself and alive for myself, then I'm not satisfied I really represent it. I enjoy trying to recreate the known person in a descriptive sense.

Does your husband review your writing before it goes out?

My husband has been a stern teacher. I think I owe my style in some measure to my husband because I think, when I was a much younger woman, I tended to run off a good deal—to like expansive, almost Germanic sentences. I liked the roll of the words, as it were. And my husband, who has excellent style himself and is a stern critic of style, brought me to the kind of simple discourse that I now use. He doesn't always read my papers. I sometimes have to call him up for a word or spelling or usage. On certain papers where I want his critical intelligence (and he knows our field well too), then I'll bother him. Otherwise he's a very busy man, and some of the stuff I write probably wouldn't be of very great interest to him.

I also have readers among our friends and colleagues, and I take their criticism very seriously. Every paper that comes out of the project has been distributed in first-draft form for criticisms. So by the time it comes to an editor, it has gone through many hands, and I'll get statements back like "This section could be better" or "This is a repetition," that sort of thing.

Not all the writers I talk with subject themselves so openly to criticisms.

Oh, we've very good at that here; we're really very helpful to one another. Also, I don't think I know anybody who is cruel with his editing. I'll tell you this, though; there *is* one form of editing that does make me angry. I've had experiences, for example, where the simple declarative sentences, which I like, did not please the editor of X journal or Y journal, and all of my simple sentences were made into compound sentences. Or a word that I have chosen with very great care was modified by the editor and a cliché put in its place. That kind of criticism I don't take very well. The criticism of good editors I have taken very well and profited from.

Can you pick an aspect of your professional career that you're most pleased with? I saw in Who's Who of American Women *that you labeled yourself an educator.*

That seemed a fair way of putting it. I can't say which I love best; there isn't one part of what I'm doing that I'd give up. And it's because I'm doing several things at once that I enjoy my work so much. I love the teaching, I love supervision, I love everything I do here. I know all the children. I'm the analytic supervisor of all the cases, all the families who come here.

How many?

In any one month we'll have 30 to 35 families. Whole families. When you work with babies, that's what happens, you know. And I think I know all of our cases very well. I'm the consultant or supervisor on nearly all the cases, and that part I simply love.

I also get tremendous satisfaction out of seeing the most fragile and the most unpromising cases develop into healthy families—and they do! And we all feel rewarded. I love the fact that I'm working with babies, which is great fun. It's like having *everything,* you know, because in our project, those of us who are too old to have babies of our own can simply borrow everybody's baby, and we can all behave like grandmothers. That's the most fun.

I also supervise in child analysis and in child psychiatry, so I have every part of my clinical interest satisfied. Then the teaching, and I think that *includes* supervision, I simply love. We have ongoing seminars within our own program that I think are especially fun for me because they are our own students with whom we're also working very closely. To watch the progress of a student from the time he enters until the end, both in supervision and in teaching, is to *really* graduate a student, and you feel great pride.

In this office, the door is open a good part of the day unless I am writing, and it means that anybody can wander in and out with an interesting piece of news for me or just sometimes sit down and cry because some of the things we see are unendurable. The students here feel a closeness to me, and it's a form of teaching that just cannot be duplicated.

You have such an enthusiasm about all your work and such feeling for it. Have you intrigued your daughter into becoming interested in these things?

Well, she loves baby work. I've intrigued her to the point that she wants very much to be a mother, which I think is the best part. And she flirted with the idea of combining pediatrics and psychology for some time. Now she sees herself as a potential lawyer, feeling that more can be done through the exercise of the law on behalf of children.

That's her present direction. Now, that can change in a year or two; one never knows. She'll be a freshman next year.

And she loves that part of my work which I could share. I could never discuss cases with my daughter, of course, since this was intimate material and she was educated from the start not to expect any answers to her questions regarding patients. She really learned confidentiality. At the same time, she would have been deprived of understanding part of my work, except that when I began work with blind babies, confidentiality was not a factor. Nobody was coming to us for psychotherapy but rather to help us in promoting the development of babies. So when Lisa was as young as four years, when Dave Freedman and I would review film on Saturday afternoon, all of our kids would come together and watch the movies. They became very discerning observers of babies. Children are sometimes so astute; they picked up small signs that we would miss, and it became a very serious Saturday afternoon entertainment for Dave's three young kids and my four-year-old.

At one point Lisa became very interested in one part of my work when we were dealing with Piaget's concept of object permanence, trying to examine the evolution of the concept of permanence in blind children. She quickly learned the Piagetian tasks, and in one of the most hilarious experiments ever conducted, she put our dumb beagle through the procedures, and of course he flunked out. He flunked out after stage four, and it became really rather a useful piece of information. I watched very closely as she consulted me on correct procedures. Even when she was sure she did not violate procedure, there was no question that the dumb dog could not pursue an object after it left his field of perception, whatever his perceptual field was. This made Lisa very sad because she thought he was smarter than that.

But it began to get us into the issue of representational intelligence in animals. When I published this as part of an object constancy paper, it became a valid way of looking at a problem. I could examine this in need states in an animal and get observations there too. And he was really not any smarter in need states than in any other area.

By the way, I had an hilarious correspondence that went on for years. I got into debate all over the country; everybody claimed his dog could do better than that. One of my colleagues said, "Everybody knows that Brandy is such a dumb dog; now my dog. . . ." So I told him to try it on his dog and report back to me. The best report I got was stage five on a golden retriever. However, there's some small evidence that our present dog, a great pyrenees, might qualify for level six: he's very smart and also has good central vision.

Was Brandy the dog you mention in The Magic Years—*the one you could always get into the basement every evening?*

Absolutely. Absolutely. And he never got any smarter.

You draw from everything around you to think and to test behavior!

Well, that's part of the fun.

Lisa has followed my work with blind children very closely. In fact, she even wrote a term paper when she was a very little girl in which she brought together what she understood of our work, using encyclopedias and other sources on the topic of blindness itself. But now mainly she is interested in babies and young children. Perhaps she sees herself as a child advocate one day.

As a matter of fact, this is one of my own concerns too because we are not only working clinically on behalf of children, working on behalf of families, we are also deeply involved in generating public concern for child welfare policies and legislation. I can't see anybody in our work today who should not be concerned, not only for psychotherapy and for intervention, but for prevention through effective social policy. There's a very good climate for this in law today, you know. And interest is going to be reflected in legislation too and in getting the attention of legislators. There is a new breed of lawyers being produced, and many have great concern for legislation and legal practice in regard to children. This is going to have an effect, I think.

Can you say a word about becoming a mother when older? You say you came late to mothering.

I was 38. I think there were many advantages. First of all, a lot of the crises of personality that simply belong in late adolescence and young adulthood should finally have been worked out within oneself. There is a readiness for full-hearted commitment to motherhood without any of the ambivalence that would have been present in the young college-age mother. A completion of one's adolescence long before—I see that as a great advantage. One disadvantage that I see is that for the child who is active, very athletic, having unathletic and, frankly, aging parents mean that there were activities that couldn't be shared in the way very young parents might. I never played baseball with my daughter, for example, or tennis. But then that may have been due as much to my own disposition as anything else.

You sound as though you have a very well-rounded and full life. Would you change anything in your life if you could?

There's one aspect of my professional development, perhaps two, that I wish I had more of. I now wish I had more training in neurology. I also wish that I had opportunities for training and fieldwork in anthropology, specifically comparative child development. This, I think, would have enlarged my life greatly. I'm only speaking professionally; there's nothing else I would want changed. I do *not* wish that I had gone to medical school; I'm glad I did not go to medical school.

In the Chess and Thomas book [1972] that reprinted your article on blind infants there appeared in large letters, "Selma Fraiberg, M.D."

Oh, that was indeed an error. I never went to medical school. I had the opportunities and simply chose not to. By that time I was teaching in medical school, and I realized that what I would need to go through was not really ever going to be applicable to what I was doing—although I now wish that I had been able to obtain more background in neurophysiology than I have.

What do you think about the thrust of the social work organizations, NASW and the like—about the so-called split between the activists and the clinicians?

I don't even know about it. I've already identified myself as one who doesn't belong to organizations. Tell me about it.

Perhaps I'm not a good one to ask. I'm not really involved in it either. But there has been established a National Federation of Societies for Clinical Social Work; there are individual societies in a number of states. They have a clinical emphasis and generally decry the falling away of graduate schools from teaching clinical skills.

Oh, that I decry too.

They seem locked in battle with the National Association of Social workers, primarily over licensing and the form licensing should take. Some clinicians feel that licensing should be restricted to master's degree social workers with a given number of years of advanced practice under supervision. The NASW model licensing bill is a multilevel bill which takes it down through the B.A. social worker and to the preprofessional level social worker. According to the clinicians, NASW has gone activist, only wanting to lobby in Washington, and they don't serve the clinical interest anymore.

I have nothing to say there, except that I think it's part of a larger trend, a tendency to abandon the social work traditions and objectives. For example, there are now schools of social work which are no longer training practitioners but are training executives, administrators, community organizers. The practice is to be conducted by graduates with a B.A., or perhaps even less. And I am simply horrified because the thing that has worried me throughout the years I have been a social worker is the tendency that began after World War II in which we moved further and further from the human center—where the patient or the client and his needs are further removed from the supervisor, administrator, policy-maker. The effect upon policy has been predictable: it has no connection with human needs at all, only imagined human needs. If you know nothing about children, how can you administer a children's program?

Are you familiar with the Council on Social Work Education's recommendation on the education of social workers?

No.

In 1971 they adopted a policy of endorsing the undergraduate degree as the entry-level practice degree for social work: the B.A. in social work would be the practice-level degree. I gather that they plan to phase out the master's, and if you want to become an administrator you would pursue the Ph.D. They have set up over 190 undergraduate sequences in social work as part of implementing that policy.

All right. I don't know what they put into these undergraduate degree sequences. I know some juniors and seniors who could probably do a very competent job upon completion of such a program, but I have no idea about what the content of these programs would be. Is it, then, the old master's degree content moved back into the undergraduate years?

It really depends on whom you train and how you train them, you see. We have undergraduates in psychology here; we bring them in as student assistants and assign them a variety of tasks—research coding, for example (but interesting coding). In the old program they were assistant observers; in the new program they participate as photographers. In order to be a good photographer in our work, you have to have an educated eye. So we have, at any one time, about four undergraduates. These are top kids who want the opportunity to see what's going on in this field.

Do you screen all the students who work here? Many of the graduate schools of social work merely present you with the students you will have in a field agency.

Oh no, we screen them. We always have about four talented juniors and seniors here; they participate in our seminars. And in addition, we provide a small stipend; they are always pleased to count that as a small bonus.

Now, knowing how good the developmental psychology courses in our school are and how good are the sequences in clinical psychology, if for these students we were to add some aspects of social work practice to this already very good existing program, resulting in a degree certification program, I think it could be possible. However, if they teach the same stuff that they're already teaching in the schools of social work but simply moving it down to the junior and senior year, I'm not so sure. But then, one could ask: "Is this, properly speaking, graduate material anyway?"

I think nothing more than family ties, metaphorically speaking, have kept me in association with social work—people I love in the field; people who hold the same values that I do; and my own staff in this project, extraordinary men and women. I think I do feel deeply committed to those values of social work which brought me into the field. Wherever they are truly represented today, I still feel identified with them.

But let me give you an example of one of our students. She was an undergraduate here, a student assistant, and she fell in love with the profession because of the social workers on our staff whom she admired so. She was one of the most talented students we've ever had—way ahead of most master's degree students—and she entered her school of social work (not here by the way) and was assigned a fieldwork placement in which she learned absolutely nothing. She was one who could judge what she had learned. She knew what she had learned in her participation here and in very good courses at the university. She has not yet had the experience which brought me into loving the beginning of my professional years, namely, good supervision. She is now going to leave her degree behind her and enter another field.

That's sad. Do you think that within social work we can bring up new Selma Fraibergs—aside from good luck and good circumstance?

Again, its the agency that matters. Go back to the very beginnings of social work when most of the training was conducted within an agency and not a school. If you remember our own origins, long before there were schools of social work there were intramural training programs within social agencies. And where I see good work being done today by social workers, it reflects the agency and the supervision they were lucky enough to get somewhere along the way. That's all there is to it. I do not see it coming out of any academic programs for social work that I know of. We have to rely on diverse and often inadequate field-work placements in such situations. Or it may be that people who are in the field and who are clinically minded will have to find their own methods of pursuing their professional goals.

And I don't know who the current leaders of the field are. I stopped reading the journals, with the exception of *Clinical Social Work Journal,* which I think is coming along promisingly. In fact, nobody here is reading them. We dutifully take all the social work journals here, and I encourage everybody to read everything. But I know they're reading in other journals; you know all the really exciting things that are going on in our field are being published elsewhere. Who the leaders are, who are the spokesmen, who are the catalysts for the examination of social work principles and its future, I don't even know.

Let me ask you about your future. You spoke earlier about retiring at some point. Tell me more about what you want after that.

I will probably retain some teaching and consultation, some small part of practice, and writing. There is much left to do. I like writing for fun. It's very relaxing to do an article for *Red Book Magazine* and the like. But the highest priority has to be for the write-up of the project, of course.

And time for travel. Maybe my old interest in anthropology can be satisfied, though it can never be fulfilled professionally. In five years perhaps, my husband will be retiring and we will be free to travel. I can see us attaching ourselves as interested laymen, because we're in a related field, to an archeological research team, let's say, or an anthropological team. Numerous things that we want to do together; we're good old traveling companions. We have lots of fun together, and we always find that travel leads to some discovery or another. And maybe I could be a visiting professor someplace, and he could be a visiting professor someplace, and we could work that out too. There is no end of fascinating things to be done!

REFERENCES

Fraiberg, S. Intervention in infancy: A program for blind infants. In S. Chess and A. Thomas (Eds.), *Annual progress in child psychiatry and child development.* New York: Brunner/Mazel, 1972.

Fraiberg, S. The muse in the kitchen: A case study in clinical research. *Smith College Studies in Social Work,* 1970, **40,** 101–134.

Fraiberg, S. The magic years. New York: Scribners, 1959.

VIRGINIA SATIR conducts seminars throughout the world on family therapy. Her major work on the subject was *Conjoint Family Therapy* (1964).

Chapter 9

VIRGINIA SATIR

On a few occasions, it's happened that when I have been talking with other professionals, your name has come up and it may come out that you're a social worker. People are always surprised. So my question is: Do you identify with social work at all?

My answer to that may be a little upsetting to some people. I believe that social work is a role and has nothing to do with my identification. I've had training in social work, but one of my biggest efforts is to try to get rid of all the delineation between social work, psychiatry, and psychology because I believe that if we are going to help people, we all have to know the same things. I'm proud of my connection with social work and that I learned my beginnings in it. I do not, at this moment in time, consider myself a social worker. I consider myself very related to it but equally related to psychiatry and to psychology. Many people—especially women—say to me how pleased they are that I'm in the field of social work. I'm glad of that.

You see, I don't want to build any boxes around me, because I don't believe that is helpful. We have too many boxes as it is. I'm proud of my base in social work, but at this point my work is not in any sense exclusively what could be called social work.

How successful have you been at breaking down barriers?
Very.

Is that because you're Virginia Satir? Do you think the average social worker, say, in a psychiatric hospital, could do that?
Sure. They do it. They've done it. You see, this has to do, it seems to me, with how you feel about yourself. I started my professional life in 1936, and I saw all kinds of ways in which professions ordered themselves in relation to each other. I think the clients paid the bill.

I remember something that happened in Chicago. I could not believe it. I had a private practice and saw a couple. They didn't have very much money, so I did the workup and so on, and I referred them to one of the clinics. Well, two things happened. One was that the clinic people told me they couldn't take the case because it was a marital problem (this was back in the forties), so they should get their marital problem fixed up and then they could come back and get individual therapy. And two, they said this case should only be handled by a psychiatrist. The result, of course, was they didn't get any help. This meant two things to me: The first is that when things get a label, then they can only be handled by so and so. And secondly, the idea that only "deep therapy" can help individuals. Its just a bunch of nonsense as far as I'm concerned. I don't think that any form of treatment guarantees anything. It's always in the hands of who does it.

In terms of my identification, I could never buy the idea that only these things could go on over here and those things go on over there, when they were all problems relating to people.

When you think about services, social workers are the ones who have got the most experience with people's problems, with people's living problems. They know more about this than anybody, but they have been the least willing to talk about it. My respect and my admiration for what social workers have been able to do is very high. What I'm trying to do is help them to see what fantastic experiences they have and how they can do a great deal to make this world better. This world is not, at this moment in time, a particularly healthy place for human beings.

At present, I do not identify myself with any one discipline. I call myself a human educator. I even would like to get rid of the word "therapy." I think that therapy is one form of human education. So for me, the whole thrust of what is now called therapy is toward better human education.

As long as I'm on my horse, I'd like to get rid of the mental health concept too, and I'll tell you why. The fact that you're not sick doesn't mean you're healthy. Just like the fact that you're not sad doesn't mean that you're anything; it only means that you're not sad. In my opinion, what really goes into the health of human beings is growth. Total growth. For me, that goes under the umbrella of human education. We are just beginning to think that maybe our priorities ought to be in human education.

You were talking about social workers doing significant work. Do you feel there's a low self-esteem problem there?

Horrible, horrible! I can go back 30 years when the social worker felt like the handmaiden to psychiatry. The other thing was that the social worker could do "the simple things," which always drove me out of my tree. The psychiatrist could see the kid, and the social worker was supposed to see the parents—but that's the most difficult part!

I have heard family therapists use that concept of therapy as education. I've heard you and Andrew Ferber say that, so I have the feeling that you latched onto that first. Is that so? Why?

Well, I can answer you this way. People who go into family therapy do begin to see this. You see, mankind has performed as he went along, using the best he knew how.

Even though I can look back and I talk about certain things that drive me out of my tree, I also have to remember that there were only certain kinds of information available at that time. We didn't have access to the kinds of things then that made us know there were other places to look.

Most of the family therapists I know, and those who have been in it any length of time at all, have begun to realize the first point that I made: that whoever helps people has to have the same information. Further, what is going on in families is a microcosm of the world. The family can be viewed in terms of a world context. Who lives in any community but children who have grown big doing what they've learned?

That's a great big leap because once you've realized that, then you can't do any of this departmentalization any more. You have to look at the fact that we haven't had a priority about people. We had a strong psychology about getting rid of problems. This is why I want to get rid of the concept of mental health. Most people-helpers have been trained for mental ill health. We don't yet know that much about health.

Those of us who really have seen the family have seen a totality that is different from what we were able to see before. It doesn't make us better. It only means that by seeing a family day in and day out, one begins to be aware of things that one could not be aware of as an individual therapist—you couldn't even be aware of as a group therapist—because you couldn't see all of the pieces.

If we all need the same information, what, in your opinion, should be the basic entry level? Are you one of these people who believe you either have it or you don't, whatever "it" is?

I certainly do not believe we're born prepared to become therapists. We had to learn it. It's harder for some of us than for others to be able to use ourselves that way.

I'm not impressed with what I see in education because I don't see training for the evolution of a person in the professional schools. I see them training for techniques and for categories, and I see nothing that says much about people being human beings. For instance, I don't see much that relates to the human soul. Here and there are some exceptions, such as the University of Nevada Medical School. There's an outstanding example of training people for people, not for illness or for symptoms or making the therapist mainly into a technician.

At the same time, I can be sympathetic, because we've been slowly struggling our way through. It seems to me quite obvious that both the people who go to be trained and what they've trained for need to include the priority of what people are about. There are startling discrepancies. I hear a class in some professional school talking about rapport, and there's no rapport in the class. If I'm a teacher and I'm teaching about relationships, and in my classroom I do not have any relationships, how can I give a living, breathing experience as a model?

But there are guilds in this field—medicine, psychology, social work. You just can't come in and say: Now we're all going to be educators; we're all going to share the same knowledge.

You see, even the word educator is contaminated, so we have to have something else. Let's take a look at something. If we waved a magic wand and said, "Now we will all be human educators," there would be chaos. If we look at present-day therapy on an evolutionary basis—and I feel sympathetic toward the process of evolvement—the following becomes apparent. Social work grew out of ladies of the past who cared about people who were suffering and brought them baskets of food and medical supplies and so forth; psychiatry grew out of helping people who were really very crazy and wondering what to do about it; psychology grew out of how to measure intelligence. All had different roots. Over the years, what's been happening? Each discipline has been discovering more and more about how to work effectively.

Let's see. Social work, as I think of it, probably had its roots in the beginning of the nineteenth century. The first juvenile court in Chicago was established in 1899. In the process of developing, they too found that one of the things they had to do was not just to take care of people but to help people take care of themselves. Unfortunately, social workers then got off the track and seemed directed toward becoming junior psychiatrists by the middle of the forties.

All the early stuff of clinical psychology was in terms of testing, trying to figure out what the brain was all about. It began to become clear that the brain couldn't function without the rest of the body, and so they got into the whole business of what makes a person able.

Psychiatry had its roots in medicine. It would be difficult for any doctor to miss emotional manifestations which at one time were looked upon as purely physical manifestations.

Wherever one started, when you look deeper you find that we're all ending up at the same point whether we like it or not. We're ending up at the point where people are moved by their perceptions, by their beliefs, by the way in which they're integrated and how they live. I respect the idea that our past experience has something to do with what happens right now. We've been moving closer because of the discoveries of what we were trying to do— because all three of these professions were interested in creating change, trying to get to some other point, trying to do something about keeping society safe, like rehabilitating criminals or getting sick people well or something of that sort.

I don't want to leave out nursing and the clergy, because I think they also play a part. Evolvement in these fields has brought people to what you hear about all over now: teamwork.

Now, when we talk about something—I think this may be related to what you were saying—how do I know I'm me? I'm me if I can say I'm a psychologist or a doctor, or. . . .

Get a credential.

Yes. OK. When we flip that around and I find that I'm me, not because I'm a this or a that, which is only a role anyhow, but because I am a person, then we come to a place where—were we to start joining all the information we have in the interest of the health of people—we would become builders together. At this point, we don't yet have in society enough of the feeling of value or enough experience with what it means to be builders. We have more experience in being competitors. So, to take the role concept further, for me to be anything, I've got to have that fancy name, and not only that: I have to have one different from you. That's beginning to change a little. We are getting more aware of what building could be between people. Since the time of Christ, I think, we have had only two ways to solve problems: capitulate or attack. These solutions were primarily based upon the idea that for me to be anything, I have to have myself defined from outside me—my money, my credentials, my status. I'm nothing without that, you know. That's what they say.

Do you care about credentials?

No. That's why I can talk to you about paraprofessionals. That's getting into the whole peer thing. I believe that we're going into a new set of guidelines about what makes it possible for people to be let loose on society. I would no more look in the yellow pages to find a psychologist, a social worker, or a doctor to heal me than I would go to the moon. Well, maybe I could go to the moon easier, I don't know.

If you needed a doctor, how would you find him?

What I would do is ask around among my friends. If I were in a completely strange place, I would call the Medical Society.

But that's for physical sciences. Suppose you needed a therapist, you had a personal problem.

If I needed a therapist, I'd go through the same route to find somebody. I'd ask my friends. I'd find somebody who would find somebody who would tell me.

You wouldn't look for High Church credentials somewhere because you felt you had to go to a psychiatrist? That's how you could get your insurance to pay.

No, because there's not necessarily any relationship between the credential and the competence of a person. That's sad, but it's so. You know that; that's not new. I don't know if we're going to change it. All I'm saying is that I don't think there's any necessary relationship in terms of the degree we get, the credential, or that it is a comment on our competence as a human being.

You know what I think? I think you don't mind being in a state of flux.

Not at all. In fact, is there any other way you can be? Because isn't change always happening? So it's a matter of acknowledging it and being with it instead of behaving as though it really isn't there.

Well, it depends. It's the way to be if growth interests you or change doesn't frighten you. But how many people could tolerate that? Some could experience it, I imagine, as anxiety.

Of course. A lot of people think they can hang on. Do try to hold on to this minute, please. It doesn't matter what you do, how much you love, how much you hate. This minute has gone by and its going to be the next minute, no matter what you do. Some people act like they could hang on to time, you see. But that is being out of harmony with a natural process.

How come? Do you know?

I don't know that I know anything. I only have ideas.

Well, do you have any idea why it's out of harmony?

Sure. Because of what we teach about how people are. We teach people that there is a right way—that there's only one power, and that somebody else has got it. And the way they can get their feeling of worth is to please somebody else. So, what we have are people who are constantly on the guilt/hostility axis or a dependent/independent axis and moving back and forth, and so there's no inner peace.

Let's go back to family therapy and its origins. I want to tell you about a thought I have. And I wonder if you think there's anything to it, and if so, what? I started in social work in the early fifties, and the most popular term then, which I'm sure you've heard of, was the schizophrenogenic mother. Remember?

I heard that, but that was in the days of immaculate conception, because there were no fathers.

Family therapy came into being somewhere in the latter part of the fifties. Is that correct?

Well, more or less. I started in '51.

You may have started your work then, but you didn't articulate it for a while.

Oh no, I was working in the basement. I didn't think anyone knew anything about it. But anyway, it turned out that a lot of other people were there at that time too, but go ahead.

Family therapy did initiate a shift from looking at the mother as the sick parent to "Let's look at everything." And Women's Lib wasn't around then. Did you feel repulsed at that notion?

I knew that was there, and I knew there was another word, momism, which is the same thing. It meant that the woman was the central point of the universe and, for that, she should get all the credit. Momism was the credit side; schizophrenogenic was the debit side. OK? So what it turned out to be, woman was the center of all things. That, however, was not for me. It was something that I didn't believe, but in those days everything was fancied up by psychoanalytic terms. You know, there's not one kind of emotion you can have that doesn't get fancied up. Like, nobody was ever angry, they were always hostile. You could never want to get invitations from soembody; you always had to be seductive. So we ran into a whole contamination of that.

The big reason for my getting into family therapy was an accident plus another thing. One of the beautiful things I got from my family, particularly my mother, was that I could question anything—that the word of somebody else was a nice thing, but it wasn't necessarily law. Typically, I would always look, and if things didn't fit, no matter how many people told me they were supposed to fit, I would let go of all that stuff and would try to see what I could do to make them fit.

And you let go of that?

Absolutely. I never could stand being in boxes. Because from the time I was very young, I seemed to believe that hypotheses were always things you started out with, but you changed them when you found new facts. I could never stand orthodoxy. I can't to this day, and I don't honor it at all. If it fits, I can use it. If it doesn't, then I have to change it. That's what I've been doing—not to fit my whims but to fit what I was finding.

What I saw was what I saw, but I always knew there was more. I didn't know what it was, but I was willing to look and see what else there was. I treated myself much as an explorer in an uncharted sea. I was willing to go there: I didn't know what I'd find, but I was willing to go. I didn't have enough sense at that time. What I mean is, I didn't have fears about what I'd find or rules that I shouldn't find it. So it made sense to me to find out whatever there was.

The real push for me was that I went into private practice in the 1940s. I got all the patients that someone else had gone through the full, orthodox analytic business with, and they hadn't changed. At first I thought: "So who am I to take people that Tom French, Gerhardt Piers and other people worked over and nothing had happened?" Certainly I couldn't do it the same way? I had only analytic theory. I had a long analysis myself. I knew about all that. Something else was needed. I knew that this wouldn't work, so I just looked. What I found was all accidental. I could claim no credit, and still can't and probably never will, for knowing where I can go. I only know I can start on the journey of exploration with open eyes. Then I can see what's there that's new. I don't know why that is, but I'm not afraid to go ahead. I go one foot at a time, little by little.

I had this young woman who had the label of ambulatory schizophrenia. That was also a popular term then, which meant you could be crazy and still walk around. Things had been going well in the treatment. One day I got a telephone call from her mother saying she would sue me for alienation of affection. Whatever happened that day— luck, accident, chance, or whatever—I heard two messages in her voice: one was a threat, the other was a plea. I answered the plea. I said, "Come on in. Let's look at this." The mother came in and I said to myself, "What's cooking here?" My patient was right back where she was when I had first seen her. So I started looking. I knew she had a father. So I asked her to let him come, and I saw another picture. I just kept looking; I was crawling in the dark. It turned out also she had a brother, and finally I had the whole family there. Then I began to see something I had never seen before. This was the beginning of what I now call systems thinking.

The kinds of problems I worked on were then called schizophrenic. And at that time, people didn't think much could happen with people who had that label. What I really saw in people's problems was the outcome in the extreme of low self-esteem and all that went with that. I had a big laboratory to work in which nobody else cared about. Nobody fought to get schizophrenic patients. Few people believed that anything could happen. As a consequence, nobody bothered me. I could work and experiment freely. Out of this, I learned some important things.

I started teaching at the Illinois Psychiatric Institute in 1955, which is where psychiatrists trained. I taught something called Family Dynamics. Out of a clear blue sky one day, somebody called me up in the office, said he had heard what I was doing and would I come to the institute and teach what I was doing. I didn't think anybody knew what I was doing. That was the beginning of my new directions.

Things were waking up in other places—slowly to be sure. People were beginning to question wholesale application of the psychoanalytic approach. The War demanded new approaches to restore fighting men. Really, we were seeing something that alarmed us. People were ready to at least admit some other possibilities for treatment approaches. That broke the back—maybe not the back, but the real hold of the orthodox psychoanalytic approach.

Why? Why do you think it broke the back of the psychoanalytic movement? Did you feel that it had no relevance?

That's right. The lack of relevance, the need for something else. You couldn't fight death on this scale in psychoanalysis. By the way, I want to make a distinction between what Freud contributed and what was made of it, because it's the orthodox part of this that is wrong, just like with Christianity. I often say I see a difference between Christ and Christianity; I'm on the side of Christ. I see a difference between Freud and Freudianism; I was on the side of Freud. So really what I'm talking about is the orthodoxy again.

You see, that's an interesting question for us. How does it happen that something has usefulness at the beginning, in its youth, and then gets frozen in time and starts to be imitated and then becomes the law? I mean, that's what orthodoxy is. I think it has to do with the need of people to find out how to do it and, at the same time, not feeling that they have anything creative to offer. The best they can get is what's there, and that slowly freezes everything into a hard rock. And then, of course, when someone starts deviating, all those people can say, "Look, you're leaving the fold." When Karen Horney and Melanie Klein evolved, leaving orthodoxy, a lot of people had a lot of negative things to say. But the objectors were people who would not work on their growth, so they built only on what they had. Harry Stack Sullivan was another one who left orthodoxy. And interestingly enough, of course, later on they were all looked upon favorably. But while it's going on, how can you deviate from God, so to speak? I think, and here is where the low self-worth comes in, people with high self-worth can look at what's there and add what they need. People with low self-worth have to find what's there and hang on to it because there won't be anything else. That's what orthodoxy is to me.

What did you get from your own family that helped you go in the directions you have gone?

Well, I told you the first thing, which was extremely valuable. My mother's stock answer on anything I'd like to do, as far back as I can remember, was: "Well, try it. Let's see what could happen." My mother was a remarkably creative woman. She could take things that looked like nothing, and before long they were something. She was a fantastic seamstress. We grew up on a farm. It was a nice farm and all that, but then we got into the Depression. My mother saw to it that we all looked like a fashion plate. She made dresses out of men's suits. She embroidered them and they were all chic.

How many were there?

Five. I'm the oldest. OK, so I got that attitude of there are no limits except what you can see and what you can do. Another thing was that I was brought up with a positive idea of God. There were no punishing gods in the house. That left me free.

Then there was another thing, but this was something that was negative for me, horribly negative, but turned out to be a blessing in many ways. You see, I was already this big when I was 11. I also was very precocious: in fact, I started college just before I was 15. I didn't know from nothing, except I had a beautiful zest for learning. I lived it, and because I knew how to be good, I had nice relations with people—not necessarily intimate, but good. I loved learning. I still love it to this day. And so I ate up everything, everything around, but I was also very young. But the thing I was going to comment on—being this tall at age 11 meant that I had no competition. No, I never had to compete for anything. It was always a matter of finding spaces for myself. You have no idea how hard it was to find a size 11 shoe for an 11-year-old kid that looked like a kid's shoe. It was a monumental thing.

Where were you at this time?

It was in Wisconsin, and my mother had made a vow unto herself that when I was ready for high school, she would move into the city. We went to Milwaukee as I got ready because she wanted a good school for her kids.

She was a beautiful, magnificent woman who only went to the fourth grade, at least in formal school. She was a remarkable seamstress, and her specialty was sewing beautiful clothes for crippled people. She padded clothes —no matter what the crippling was in the body, she made them look fabulous. I would see some of those people come, and of course a lot of the doctors in the city or other people would send them to my mother for their clothes. She knew how to do all kinds of marvelous things. Anyway, my mother's feeling about education was very strong. All her kids got a college education or beyond.

Where did that come from? Was it cultural, religious?

Well, the female side of our family comes from German royalty, so I had that "royal" background. These women didn't have very good sense, because they got involved with "low-caste" men and that wasn't so good. There was a combination of the queen and the scullery maid. That's what I also had to deal with. Elegance, smartness, an ability to work hard—Cinderella style. They fought lots of times. Can't you imagine?

My father was a beautiful man, but he never really got into his own ability. He was a mathematical genius. He could do fantastic things with his hands, he could figure all kinds of things in his head. He was the last of 13 children; his mother had two sets of twins. They were pioneers. I was born in the same house my father was born in. We were all born there. There was that link in that heavy pioneer background. I heard the stories of my grandfather having to pull the tree stumps out and the heavy work that went on. My grandfather was a young man when they came to that country. The pioneer bit was very close to me too.

It's an interesting mixture.

Well, it shows. I have now made friends with all those parts and evolved them so that they're at least in good shape. I can still work very hard in all kinds of ways, but it now has a rhythm and a harmony. I have worked a long time to achieve it.

Another interesting thing, I think, was that I was sick on and off from the time I was five until I was 35. Between five to 14—I was deaf for two years during that period. I had a very serious operation and I was declared dead when I was 5½ years old. You see, I grew up in a Christian Science background with my mother; my father was very opposed to it. I learned to feel my body and to believe that the health of it was related to how I felt. That was one piece of it. The other piece was, whenever anything went wrong with my body, I also felt that there was something wrong with me. When all the physical things came up with me, there was always a big fight in the family; I was the only child who was sick so much. I was the first child. Now that I know something about family systems, I know what was going on.

What was going on?

What was going on was that my father and my mother had this basic disagreement that started to develop when I got appendicitis when I was 5½ years old. My mother's feeling was to get a Christian Science practitioner. My father's way of dealing with that was to try to get me to the hospital. And they argued for three weeks and peritonitis set in. At one point, I remember being in the Morris chair and hearing all this. I was delirious and my father grabbed me and took me to the hospital, which was 19 miles away. I remember vaguely being in his arms, going up the steps. And this I didn't hear, but he told me the doctor felt my pulse and there wasn't any. Well, I guess in those days they didn't know there were seven stages to dying—six maybe —so he insisted they operate. I was a long time in the hospital. I still have a huge scar.

Did they know you had appendicitis?

I don't know what they knew. I only know I was terribly ill. Anyway, the myth of it was that my mother wanted to kill me and my father saved me. Well, I didn't believe either one of those, but I also couldn't believe this other stuff.

Later, my mother was pregnant with her last child, my brother Ray. So her pregnancy, my being in the hospital, my father being angry—I did a convenient thing psychologically: I got deaf. A mastoid set in and there was no medical treatment. So it just did whatever it did and destroyed one eardrum completely, so I was deaf for two years. And why my hearing came back, my mother said, was because of God; my father said it was accidental. Nevertheless, I had limited hearing in one ear, and in 1964 I had eardrum grafts to cure the condition.

There was another interesting thing that came out of that: it was almost as if I was invulnerable, no matter what happened. At 18, I was out in the lake swimming. For whatever reason, I almost drowned and was practically dead again. So there was a kind of invulnerability too. You know—whatever would happen, I would come through it. This also had a positive side to it: it meant I had very little fear about doing anything—stepping off. I'd be real careful about it, but the unknown didn't hold many dangers.

What happened at age 35? Because apparently things were different after that.

Yes. Well, other things happened after all that other mess. I had braces on my legs because I had weak ankles. So as a result, in my childhood I didn't do too many of the childhood fun things because I wasn't able to.

At 35 I had stomach trouble. All the time, I had stomach trouble. I know now that too was a whole vulnerable area. I went into analysis at that time, and that helped me to begin to get some messages straight. But what it didn't help me with was my relationship to men and myself as a person. I had a very good analyst, but it just wasn't enough. Yet it was what I needed to start; it was the beginning of my looking at me. I needed parts of me to be integrated— parts that I knew must be there, but I didn't know what they were. By this time, you know, I was a full-fledged professional. And my own feeling that there had to be more than being integrated and what my analysis was giving me led me to look in that area too.

You seem to be saying: "Yes, analysis did help in terms of expanding myself." What I don't understand is what you felt you lacked.

Oh, all the things relating to men, being a sexual woman. None of that got touched. You see, I realized that since everything had to come out of me and no input was there, then there were whole areas I couldn't possibly get into because I didn't even know about them myself. I was always competent, supercompetent. And the only place anxiety showed was in physical symptoms. So when the physical symptoms disappeared, integration was made around that kind of thing.

But my belief is, we have to be whole in terms of the sex that we are. Our personhood and sexism mean we have to be able to integrate someone who is the other sex. And this is purely and completely, for the most part, a learning from what we see between our parents. You see, I began the process but I didn't finish it. I didn't know I didn't finish it about my parents being people, but there was so much that just didn't happen. I got more depressed after the analysis. Very depressed. And after all those thousands of dollars and what not, I knew that there had to be much more that could happen.

So it sounds like you continued your journey yourself. Did you feel that you accomplished the part that you didn't get in analysis, and how was that done?

The same thing that I did before: a little bit of just keep going, looking for what's there.

Let me tell you how that happened. In my looking, I was seeing patients. I was a therapist all this time, and I see patients with an open mind and I see things I need to do. I didn't know anything about gestalt therapy. One day, for instance, somebody was watching me and said, "You must have been studying with Fritz Perls." And I said, "Who's that?" He said, "A Gestaltist." I said, "What is that?" And he said, "Well, you're doing it." I arrived at gestalt by looking at the internal dialogue that a person had with his self-worth and being able to deal with that. So I thought, "Well, if there is something like that around, I'd better go find out."

One day I was working and somebody said, "Oh, you must have studied Korzybski." "Who's that?" "Oh, he's a general semanticist." "Why?" "Well, you're doing it." "Very interesting. So I'll go and find out about him." Then I developed something in family reconstruction, and someone said to me, "Oh, psychodrama." No, I never studied psychodrama. But you see the elements that were there in this search for finding, not only pieces, but to make those pieces fit, was like someone else's work. Then I would go and find out.

And then, of course, I always was interested in the spiritual. The mystical, the spiritual, the parapsychological: they all had something in common with one another.

Are you a religious person now?

Very, I think. I've always been a religious person, but not with a capital R. I belong to no church. Churches get too orthodox for me. I cannot think.

Were you raised Christian Scientist?

And German Lutheran, both.

They never did settle that argument.

No. So what did I do at the age of 17? I made a study of all the religions of the world. So I find out a very interesting thing—that all the religions of the world are doing two things: trying to regulate man's relationship to man and help him explain his relationship to the universe. And they all have different ways of doing it. In relating man's relationship to man, they tried to give recipes for how it should be done. OK, so the recipes differ, but that's the basic underpinning.

Who has been most influential in your life? I'm sure your mother, from what you've said. But are there any other people that you feel you owe a great deal to?

I owe a lot to my mathematics teacher in high school. Beautiful, lovely, Estelle Stone. An ordinary-looking woman and most marvelous. And then to several of my teachers in college. I think what must have happened is they saw this young, knock-kneed kid who had a big brain, who had gone around acting like a grownup, and whom they knew didn't know from borscht. And since I was bright, and since I was someone who loved to learn—that was just peeking out of me all over—all the people who could connect with that were helping me.

And then there were five people in a geography book. When I was only nine years old, there was a picture of a very black-skinned person, a red-skinned person, a yellow-skinned person, a brown-skinned person, and a white-skinned person. I looked, and I'll never forget it. It is like it was yesterday. I looked, and here I am in a little farming community. Everywhere I went, everybody had white skin —mostly German, some Polish—and I wanted to find out about these other people.

I want to ask you about men and women. Has being female been a problem for you? Do you get a lot of tokenism?

Not that I know of. But you see, there might be and I wouldn't know it. I think I got spared a lot of that because I never became competitive. I respect men and I like men, but I often felt sorry for them. And that goes right back to my family. My mother would be bitchy to my father, and I'd see his face and I'd feel horrible. And then, when he'd run off and do something he wasn't supposed to, I'd get mad as hell with him. I favored, very much, in appearance, my father. And as far as my relations with men were concerned, it never bothered me to help them. But I never helped in any overt kind of way.

I have lived in a world of men because I'm much more related to psychiatric medicine than I am with anything else. It just happened that way. I have had many psychiatrists who have learned from me, and a lot of my work abroad is heavily medical and male. Some men have tried to put me down. Nobody gets very far with that because I don't respond to it much. I could be a little hurt over it, but that's all. Sometimes I feel, when I go to some meetings, that men like to make me into their little doll and reduce me, which is a sexual response.

But there's always a lot of respect. You see, I've never been in any place where I would be a token thing. And a lot of times I am referred to as the "great mother" or the "white witch"—things like that.

But now let's turn that a little bit around in terms of my own romantic relations. I made two marriages: one was a war marriage which hardly lasted two months and the other was a longer one. But when it came to a personal thing, I had that idea of being the one to take care of the male, and then I would feel isolated. I didn't know how to be alone, and I couldn't stand it. I didn't know then, but I learned a lot since.

So I suppose, until relatively recently, I did feel a sense of being unwhole because I wasn't related to a man over a long period of time. And now I've worked myself into a position where marriage is impossible because I'm running around all the time. But I can do it freely because now it feels right to me. If marriage were to happen now, it would be like two people coming together instead of half a person coming to another half and making one whole.

In your book, Peoplemaking, *you have a quote from* The Prophet—*the one about marriage that says "the pillars of the temple stand apart." And of course therein is a paradox. Would you like to expand on that some more? Why does separateness, aloneness, make us close? And why is the opposite so dangerous, the inability to be alone?*

It goes that togetherness is the ability to come and go without guilt or blame. OK. That's where you start off; that's against togetherness, which implies commitment and that you stick together all the time, as compared to, "If I separate from you, it means I don't love you." So part of that has to do, on the belief level, with the freedom to come and go without guilt.

Oftentimes that's understood to allow all kinds of free action outside—like sleep with whomever you want or do anything you want. You see, it's freedom that gets misunderstood. It's license, not freedom.

You don't buy that at all?

No, not at all. Because I think freedom carries its responsibilities. License carries none. I don't know how one could live without responsibility, because in this world there's always you and me. And what I do affects you; what you do affects me. The question is how do we work out the negotiations?

Another thing that's implied when two people are tied to a single objective from time to time—that is, how to spend the same pot of money, what to do together with time, and things you bring together, like children, etc. If I feel that you, in your caring as my mother or my daughter or whatever, can make my life better, it's also possible for me to make your life better. Not because I make decisions for you or take away from myself in order to do that, but in the kind of contribution we can make to each other through our expression to each other, through what we can give each other, and what we can state to each other about our boundaries so we have two real people together.

So I made this little picture. I have two people on swivel chairs. You turn in your swivel chair. You live in your own world and the other one lives in his own world. Now, there's a third world, and that comes from the two worlds. It isn't that only one world exists; all three have to exist. That takes constant negotiation. It takes constant evolving. It takes being up to date in your communication. It takes the freedom to be real—all of which, for the most part, are new skills, new beliefs for people.

There's a strong implication that commitment and love means ownership and capitulation. I've been able to help a lot of people to get real freedom and to grow while nurturing their mutual world because I had a strong feeling that their third world would be nothing unless each of the two worlds had contributed to it—contributed from their own internal assets.

When each person felt firm on his own feet and felt free to negotiate, then each developed a different kind of trust. They could both grow, and they were constantly giving to each other in some kind of way, but on the basis of realness, not on the basis of power.

You never did say what your first career was; you said social work was your second.

At first, I didn't know whether or not I wanted to teach, so I started teaching. I was a demonstration teacher before I got out of college. I loved working with kids. I had a degree to work with exceptional children, secondary-school age. I didn't want to stay in any school system very long, so I didn't. I taught six years in five schools.

What prompted you to get the social work degree?

Well, it was very clear to me very shortly. I was aware that I wanted to learn more about people. I felt, the first day of school, that it was inconceivable that I wouldn't want to know the children's families. Nobody in teacher's training told me anything about that. On the first day of school, I would say: "I'd like to know your families. Who wants to take me home with you?" One little black child said, "I want to." When he opened the door, his mother said, "The first day of school and he's already done something wrong!" But every night I went, and I had 42 kids in the classroom so it took me a little over two months to get to every kid in the room. I rarely had behavior problems with my kids. We did all kinds of fantastic things because we were all one big family. But it just seemed that was the thing to do. Nobody told me.

Your mistake was in not asking what the system wanted you to do.

I'd never do it and I never will. I always say what I'm going to do, and I always do it. I say, "Look, isn't it fun?" and nobody says, "No, it isn't fun." You see, I don't believe I've asked permission from anyone for anything. That doesn't mean I bulldoze my way in. But I don't want to insult anybody by asking them to be in possession of information that I know they don't have. So I will work at what I think is the highest level and explain what I want to do and ask them if they can help me. If they can't help me, then they can say so. I wouldn't think of asking, because the natural response to asking permission is "no." That's so you'll be on the safe side. I wouldn't put anybody in such a terrible spot.

The safe side?

Sure. You're on the safe side because at least you won't make anything terrible. I wouldn't treat anyone like that.

REFERENCE

Satir, V. *Peoplemaking.* Palo Alto, Ca.: Science and Behavior Books, 1972.

BIBLIOGRAPHY

Addams, J. Ethical survivals in municipal corruption. *International Journal of Ethics*, April 1898, 273–279.

Addams, J. *The spirit of youth and the city streets.* New York: Macmillan, 1909.

Addams, J. *Twenty years at Hull House.* New York: Macmillan, 1909.

Addams, J. Aspects of the women's movement. *Survey*, Aug. 1, 1930, 384–410. (a)

Addams, J. *The second twenty years at Hull House.* New York: Macmillan, 1930. (b)

Alexander, L. Social work's Freudian deluge: Myth or reality? *Social Service Review*, 1972, *46*, 517–538.

Brown, G. E., Ed. *The multi-problem dilemma.* Metuchen, N.J.: Scarecrow Press, 1968.

Flugel, J. C. *Psychoanalytic study of the family.* London: International Psycho-analytical Press, 1921.

Fraiberg, S. Intervention in infancy: A program for blind infants. In S. Chess and A. Thomas (Eds.), *Annual progress in child psychiatry and child development.* New York: Brunner/Mazel, 1972.

Fraiberg, S. The muse in the kitchen: A case study in clinical research. *Smith College Studies in Social Work*, 1970, *40*, 101–134.

Fraiberg, S. *The magic years.* New York: Scribners, 1959.

Hollis, F. *Casework: A psychosocial therapy.* New York: Random House, 1964.

Johnson, E. *Jane Addams, A centennial reader.* New York: Macmillan, 1960.

Lasch, C. *The new radicalism in America, 1889–1963.* New York: Knopf, 1965.

Perlman, H. H. Confessions, concerns and commitment of an ex-clinical social worker. *Clinical Social Work Journal,* 1974. *2,* 221–229.

Perlman, H. H. *Perspectives in casework.* Philadelphia: Temple University Press, 1971.

Perlman, H. H. *Persona: Social role and personality.* Chicago: University of Chicago Press, 1968.

Perlman, H. H. *Social casework: A problem-solving process.* Chicago: University of Chicago Press, 1957.

Redl, F. and Wineman, D. *Controls from within: Techniques for the treatment of the aggressive child.* New York: Free Press, 1952.

Redl, F. and Wineman, D. *Children who hate.* New York: Free Press, 1951.

Richmond, M. *Social diagnosis.* New York: Russell Sage Foundation, 1922.

Satir, V. *Peoplemaking.* Palo Alto, Ca.: Science and Behavior Books, 1972.

Satir, V. *Conjoint family therapy.* Palo Alto, Ca.: Science and Behavior Books, 1964.